State Laws and Regulations Governing Newborn Screening

Compiled by

Lori B. Andrews, J.D.

Research Attorney and Project Director, American Bar Foundation

Chicago American Bar Foundation 1985

This monograph was made possible by a grant, Project Number MCJ-173380-01-1, from the Division of Maternal and Child Health, U.S. Department of Health and Human Services. The authors would like to thank the following people who aided in the intricate analysis of the provisions of the states' laws: David Blake, Kathryn Herrmann, Cynthia Fruchtman, John Hendricks, and Christine Scobey.

Additional copies of this monograph are available from the National Center for Education in Maternal & Child Health, Georgetown University, 3520 Prospect, N.W., Washington, D.C. 20057.

(202)625-8400.

Library of Congress Catalog Card Number: 85-071872

ISBN 0-910059-04-7

Contents

The Reach and Substance of State Newborn Screening Laws

By **Lori B. Andrews**

Research Attorney and Project Director, American Bar Foundation

Each year, state-sponsored programs screen millions of newborn infants for various metabolic disorders. The procedures for accomplishing this public health feat are set forth on a state-by-state basis in newborn screening statutes adopted by state legislatures and regulations promulgated by state departments of health. These legal guidelines vary considerably from one jurisdiction to another in their level of detail, their substantive provisions and the types of disorders they address. This book presents a comparative overview of the provisions, followed by individual analyses of each state's laws and regulations, a description of related sickle cell screening laws and a chart of disorders for which screening is supposed to occur.

Mandatory or Voluntary Nature of Screening

Forty-eight states and Washington, D.C. have statutes governing newborn screening.[1] The statutes of three jurisdictions clearly provide the screening program is voluntary.[2] In 5 states (Arkansas, Iowa, Michigan, Montana and West Virginia), screening is mandatory and there is no provision for parental objection or refusal based on religious grounds.[3] In 31 states, the test may be refused on religious grounds only.[4]

1. **Ala.** Code §22-10A-1 §22-20-3 (1984); **Alaska** Stat. §18.15.200 (1981); **Ariz.** Rev. Stat. Ann. §36-694B (Supp. 1983); **Ark.** Stat. Ann. §§82-625, 82-626 (Supp. 1983); **Cal.** Health and Safety Code §309 (West Supp. 1984); **Colo.** Rev. Stat. §25-4-801 et seq. (1982), §25-4-1001 et seq. (1983); **Conn.** Gen. Stat. Ann. §19a-55 (West Supp. 1984); **D.C.** Code Ann. §6-311 et seq. (1981); **Fla.** Stat. Ann. §383.14 (West Supp. 1984); **Ga.** Code Ann. §88-1201.1 et seq. (Supp. 1984); **Hawaii** Rev. Stat. §333-1 (Supp. 1983); **Idaho** Code §39-909 et seq. (1977); **Ill.** Ann. Stat. Ch. 111½, §4903 et seq. (Smith-Hurd 1983), as amended by P.A. 83-87 (1983); **Ind.** Code Ann. §16-8-6-1 et seq. (Burns 1983); **Iowa** Code Ann. §136A.1 et seq. (West Supp. 1984-1985); **Kan.** Stat. Ann. §65-180 et seq (1980); **Ky.** Rev. Stat. §214.155 (1982); **La.** Rev. Stat. Ann. §40.1299 et seq. (West Supp. 1984); **Me.** Rev. Stat. Ann. tit. 22, §1522 (1980); **Md.** Pub. Health Code Ann. §13-101 to 111 (1982); **Mass.** Ann. Laws ch. 111, §110A (Michie/Law Co-op. Supp. 1983); **Mich.** Comp. Laws Ann. §§333.5431, 333.5439 (West 1980); **Minn.** Stat. Ann. §144.125 (West Supp. 1983); **Miss.** Code Ann. §§41-21-201, 203 (1981); **Mo.** Ann. Stat. §210.065 (Vernon 1983); **Mont.** Code Ann. §50-19-201 et seq. (1983); **Neb.** Rev. Stat. §71-604.01 to 604.04 (1981), §71-645 et seq. (1981); **Nev.** Rev, Stat, §442.115 (1979); **N.H.** Rev. Stat. Ann. §132:10-a, b, c (1978); **N.J.** Stat. Ann. §26:2-110 et seq. (West Supp. 1982-1983); **N.M.** Stat. Ann. §24-1-6 (Supp. 1982); **N.Y.** Pub. Health Law §2500 et seq. (McKinney 1972), **N.Y.** Pub. Health Law §2730 et seq. (McKinney 1972); **N.C.** Gen. Stat. §143B-194 (1983); **N.D.** Cent. Code §25-17-01 et seq. (1978); **Ohio** Rev. Code Ann. §§3701.501, 502 (Baldwin 1984); **Okla.** Stat. Ann. tit. 63, §1-533, 1-534 (West Supp. 1982-1983); **Or.** Rev. Stat. §433.285 et seq. (1981); **Pa.** Stat. Ann. tit. 35, §621 (Purdon 1977); **R.I.** Gen Laws §23-13-12 (1976); **S.C.** Code Ann. §44-37-30 (Law. Co-op. Supp. 1983); **S.D.** Codified Laws Ann. §34-24-16 et seq. (1977 and Supp. 1984); **Tenn.** Code Ann. §68-5-301 et seq. (1983); **Tx.** Rev. Civ. Stat. Ann. art. 4447e §1 et seq. and e-1 §1 et seq. (Vernon Supp. 1984); **Utah** Code Ann. §26-17-21 (1976) and §26-10-6 (Supp. 1981); **Va.** Code §32.1-65 et seq. (1982 and Supp. 1984); **Wash.** Rev. Code Ann. §70.83.010 et seq. (West 1978 and Supp. 1982); **W. Va.** Code §16-22-1 et seq. (Supp. 1983); and **Wis.** Stat. Ann. §146.02 (West Supp. 1982-1983); **Wyo.** Stat. §35-4-801 (Supp. 1983). Delaware and Vermont do not have statutes addressing neonatal screening.

2. **D.C.** Code Ann. §6-314 (3) (1981); **Md.** Pub. Health Code Ann. §§13-102 (10) -109 (f) (1982); and **N.C.** Gen. Stat. §143B-195 (1983).

3. **Ark.** Stat. Ann. §86-625 (Supp. 1983); **Iowa** Admin. Code §470-4.1 (136A) (regulations); **Mich.** Comp. Laws Ann. §333.5431 (1) (West 1980); **Mont.** Code Ann. §50-19-203 (1) (1983); and **W. Va.** §16-22-3 (Supp. 1983).

In 7 states, parents may object to the test for any reason.[5] The statutes of two states allow both parental and religious objections.[6] In another state, the law empowers an agency to determine whether testing should be mandatory. In Maine, the Department of Human Services is authorized to make the program mandatory, but provision for religious objection is made.[7]

Informed Consent

Although the majority of states allow objection to screening on some grounds, very few statutes require that the parents or guardians of an infant either be told they have the right to object or be sufficiently informed so that they can choose whether or not their infant should submit to the screening. Four jurisdictions by statute require that parents be informed.[8] Ironically, North Carolina, which by statute has a voluntary program, makes no provision for informing parents. The Washington, D.C., Maryland, Wisconsin, and Wyoming laws provide both that the parents be fully informed of the test and that they be given an opportunity to object. The New Mexico law provides that the parent may object after being informed, but does not explicitly provide for informing.[9]

An additional nine states under their regulations or departmental guidelines or instructions provide for informing parents or guardians.[10] In California, the person providing prenatal care must give the pregnant woman a booklet about newborn

4. **Ala.** Code §22-20-3 (a) (1984); **Cal.** Health and Safety Code §309 (West Supp. 1984); **Conn.** Gen. Stat. Ann. §§19a-55 (b) (West Supp. 1984); **Ga.** Code Ann. §31-12-7 (a) (Supp. 1984); **Hawaii** Rev. Stat. Part I §333-1 (Supp. 1983); **Idaho** Code §39-912 (1977); **Ill.** Ann. Stat. Ch. 111½, §4905 (3) (Smith-Hurd 1983-1984); **Ind.** Code Ann. §16-8-6-1 (Burns 1983); **Kan.** Stat. Ann. §65-182 (1980); **Ky.** Rev. Stat. §214.155 (2) (1982); **Mass.** Ann. Laws ch. 111, §110A (Michie/Law Co-op. Supp. 1983); **Minn.** Stat. Ann. §144.125 (West Supp. 1983); **Miss.** Code Ann. §41-21-203 (1984); **Mo.** Ann. Stat. §210.065.4 (Vernon 1983); **Neb.** Rev. Stat. §71-604.01 (1981); **N.J.** Stat. Ann. §26:2-111 (West Supp. 1982-1983); **N.Y.** Pub. Health Law §2500-a (b) (McKinney 1972); **N.D.** Cent. Code §25-17-04 (1978); **Ohio** Rev. Code Ann. §3701.501 (B) (Baldwin 1984); **Okla.** Stat. Ann. tit. 63, §1-534 (West Supp. 1982-1983); **Or.** Rev. Stat. §433.285 (3) (1981); **Pa.** Stat. Ann. tit. 35, §621 (Purdon 1977); **R.I.** Gen. Laws §23-13-12 (1976); **S.C.** Code Ann. §44-37-30 (Law Co-op. Supp. 1983); **S.D.** Codified Laws Ann. §34-24-17 (1977); **Tenn.** Code Ann. §68-5-308 (1983); **Tx.** Rev. Civ. Stat. Ann. art. 4447e §2, and §4447e-1 §5 (Vernon Supp. 1984); **Utah** Code Ann. §26-10-6 (Supp. 1981); **Va.** Code §32.1-65 (Supp. 1983); **Wash.** Rev. Code Ann. §70.83.020 (West Supp. 1982); and **Wis.** Stat. Ann. §146.02 (3) (West Supp. 1982-1983).

5. **Alaska** Stat. §18.15.200 (f) (1981); **Ariz.** Admin. Comp. R9-14-515 (1979) (provides testing is done with consent of parent); **Fla.** Stat. Ann. §383.14 (3) (West Supp. 1984); **La.** Rev. Stat. Ann. §40.1299.1 (West Supp. 1984); **Nev.** Rev. Stat. §442.115 (4) (1979); **N.H.** Rev. stat. Ann. §132:10-c (1978); and **N.M.** Stat. Ann. §24-1-6 (A) (Supp. 1982).

6. **Colo.** Rev. Stat. §§25-4-804 (1982), §25-4-1005 (1983); and **Wyo.** Stat. §35-4-801 (c) (Supp. 1983).

7. **Me.** Rev. Stat. Ann. tit. 22, §1522 (1980).

8. **D.C.** Code Ann. §6-314 (3) (A) (1981); **Md.** Pub. Health Code Ann. §13-109 (e) (2) (1982), (Supp. 1984); **Wis.** Stat. Ann. §146.02 (3) (West Supp. 1982-1983); and **Wyo.** Stat. §35-4-801 (c) (Supp. 1983).

9. **N.M.** Stat. Ann. §24-1-6 (A) (Supp. 1982).

10. **Cal.** Admin. Code tit. 17, R. 6505 (c), (h); **Fla.** "Guidelines for the Florida Infant Screening Program" IIa (April 1981); **Iowa** Admin. Code 470-4.2 (136A); **La.** Dept. of Health and Human Resources, "Guidelines: Neonatal Screening Programs" §IIA; **Minn.** Code Agency R. §1.172 c 1(a) (1979); **Ohio** Public Health Council §3701-45-01 (c)(1),-(c)(2),-(c)(3) (Jan. 2, 1981); **Pa.** Code, Chapter 28, §28.11 (1982); **S.C.** Dept. of Health & Environmental Control, Official Instructions (1980); and **Wash.** Admin. Code §248-102-020 (2), §248-29-050 (11) (a).

11. If this does not occur, the facility where the woman delivers provides the booklet.

screening.[11] In Ohio, the hospital must provide printed material.[12] Similarly, in Pennsylvania, printed material is required to be distributed by the health care facility or practitioner responsible for care of the pregnant woman or mother. In Louisiana, the guidelines include a sample brochure to be given parents; however, the brochure may be misleading since it says the screening is required by law and does not indicate that the parents have a statutory right to object on any grounds whatsoever.[13] Similarly, the screening guidelines in Indiana require screening but make no note of the fact that there is a religious exception in the statute.[14]

In Washington, the information required to be conveyed by hospital personnel to parents is quite skimpy--only that a blood sample is to be taken in compliance with state law. (No mention is made of the fact that there is a religious exemption.) In Florida and Iowa the guidelines or regulations require advising the parent of the purpose, nature and procedures of screening before specimen collection, but they do not specify that the parents must be told that they have a right to object and must be given the opportunity to do so.[15]

In at least 32 states, there is no requirement in the statute or the regulations on newborn screening for either informing parents or obtaining their consent,[16] although the North Dakota policy statement recommends "[b]rief discussion of newborn metabolic testing by physicians and nurses with the parents."[17]

In South Carolina, even though, prior to sampling, parents are to be given information about screening and the name of the physician from whom they can receive results, the departmental instructions also state that provision of screening is covered by the consent form signed by the parents upon admission to the hospital. It is questionable whether it is advisable to have a blanket consent form be extended in that manner to cover screening services.

In Maryland, the provision extends beyond consent to screening to cover informed consent to treatment. The law provides that each participant shall be informed of the nature, cost, benefits, and risks of any therapy or maintenance program available for an affected individual.[18]

12. The material is provided by a physician or midwife for an out-of-hospital birth. If neither is present, the health commissioner of the health district in which the birth occurred provides the material.

13. **La.** Dept. of Health and Human Resources, "Guidelines: Neonatal Screening Programs" § II N (1).

14. **Ind.** State Board of Health Screening Guidelines, p. 3.

15. The Iowa regulations additionally specify that the parents be told of the consequences of treatment and nontreatment.

16. Alabama; Alaska; Arizona; Arkansas; Colorado; Connecticut; Hawaii; Idaho; Illinois; Indiana; Kansas; Kentucky; Maine; Massachusetts; Michigan; Mississippi; Missouri; Montana; Nebraska; Nevada; New Hampshire; New York; North Carolina; North Dakota; Oklahoma; Oregon; Rhode Island; South Dakota; Texas; Utah; Virginia; and West Virginia.

17. **N.D.** State Department of Health Division of Maternal and Child Health, "Newborn Metabolic Screening Policy Statement" (November 1982).

18. **Md.** Pub. Health Code Ann. §13-109 (g) (1) (ii) (1982).

Quality Assurance Measures

Some statutes or regulations provide quality assurance measures for newborn screening. In 31 states by statute, regulation or guideline,[19] there is a specification of the type of laboratory in which the tests must be done (e.g., a centralized state laboratory or an approved laboratory). The states vary in the procedures that they specify for approving laboratories. The Florida regulations, for example, include among the criteria for approving a laboratory that it participate in proficiency testing, perform screening in a minimum of 50,000 newborns annually and report results in a timely manner.[20] In the District of Columbia, the laboratory designated for newborn screening must be certified by the College of American Pathologists or the U.S. Centers for Disease Control and must regularly participate in the appropriate quality control program, or have a federal laboratory license.[21] In Iowa, the central laboratory is required to have a written quality assurance plan.[22] Some states have made specific provisions for the use of a regional laboratory[23] or out-of-state laboratory.[24] Some states even have rules establishing a procedure for withdrawing approval of a laboratory.[25]

Examples of other types of quality assurance measures include providing that follow-up tests shall be made at a laboratory approved by the department,[26] providing

19. **Alaska** Stat. §18.15.200 (e) (1981); **Ark.** Stat. Ann. §82-626 (5) (Supp. 1983); **Cal.** Health & Safety Code §309 (West Supp. 1984); **Cal.** Admin. Code tit. 17, §§6503; **Colo.** Rev. Stat. §§25-4-802 (1) (1982), 25-4-1003 (1983); 5 **Colo.** Code Reg. §1005-4 (III) (1977); **D.C.** Code Ann. §§6-313 (b), 6-316 (9) (1981); **Fla.** Admin. Code §10D-76.04 (1978); **Hawaii** Dept. of Health Admin. Rules, ch. 142 §11-142-5 (1981); **Idaho** §2-12105:02, .03 (1980); **Ill.** Ann. Stat. ch. 111½, §4904 (e) (Smith-Hurd 1983); **Ill.** Admin. Reg. §661.2 (1981); **Ind.** Code Ann. §§16-8-6-6 (a), 16-8-6-7 (2) (Burns 1983); **Iowa** Code Ann. §136A.3(4) (West Supp. 1984); **Iowa** Admin. Code §§470-4.5 (136A), -(1),-(5),-(6); 902 **Ky.** Admin. Regs. 4:030 (2); **Md.** Admin. Code §§10.38.07 (A), (B) (1975); **Me.** Dept. of Health Services, "Rules and Regulations Relating to Testing Newborn Infants for Detection of Causes of Mental Retardation" §6; 7 **Minn.** Code Agency R. 1.172 C 1 (d); **Mont.** Code Ann. §50-19-203 (3) (1983); **Neb.** Rev. Stat. §71-647 (5) (1981); **N.D.** Cent. Code §25-17-02 (1978); **N.M.** Regs. §102 (1979); **N.Y.** Admin. Code tit. 10, §69.1 (1978); **Ohio** Rev. Code Ann. §3701.501 (A) (Baldwin 1984); **Okla.** Regs (1971); 28 **Pa.** Admin. Code §28.4 (1980); **Rhode Island** Department of Health, "Newborn Screening Program Specimen Collection Schedule" 3 (1964) (covering phenylketonuria); **S.D.** Codified Law Ann. §§34-24-19 (1983) (providing for use of the state laboratory when facilities not available); **S.D.** Dept. of Health Div. of Maternal and Child Health, "Newborn Metabolic Screening Policy Statement," (November 1982); Rules of **Tenn.** Dept. of Public Health Bureau of Community Health Services Administration §1200-15-1-.02(a) (1982); **Tx.** Rev. Civ. Stat. Ann. art. 4447e §§1,-2,-2A (Vernon Supp. 1982-1983); **Va.** Code §32.1-72 (Supp. 1982-83); Regs: 3.04.01; **Wash.** Rev. Code Ann. §70.83.040 (1982); **Wash.** Admin. Code R. 248-102-020 (1980); **W. Va.** Code §16-22-2 (Supp. 1983); and **Wis.** Stat. Ann. §146.02 (2) (West Supp. 1982-83).

20. **Fla.** Admin. Code §10 D - 76.04 (b), (c), and (f).

21. **D.C.** Code Ann. §§6-313 (b), 6-316 (9) (1981).

22. **Iowa** Admin. Code §470-4.5 (6).

23. The Connecticut guidelines provide that hypothyroidism testing is to be performed at the New England Regional Laboratory at the Massachusetts Health Department. State of **Connecticut** Department of Health Services Guidelines for Screening. The **N.H.** Dept. of Health and Welfare Division of Public Health Services Bureau for the Handicapped Children, "Recommendations for Newborn Screening Specimen Collection" (March 18, 1983) indicate that testing for that state shall be done through the New England Regional Program. **N.M.** Health and Environment Dept., "Newborn Screening Regulations" §102 (July 1, 1979); and **Wyo.** Dept. of Health and Social Services, "Mandatory Screening of Newborn Infants for Inborn Errors of Metabolism," ch. 35, §4(c).

24. **Mo.** Admin. Code tit. 13 §50-143.010 (4) (c) (7) (1981) (permissible to use out-of-state lab if the other state's health officer has approved the lab and the other state has rules at least as stringent as Missouri's); and **N.M.** Stat. Ann. §24-1-6B (Supp. 1982).

25. 5 **Colo.** Code Reg. 1005-4 (III) (1) (e) (1977).

26. **Alaska** §18.15.200 (e) (1981); and **Cal.** Health and Safety Code §309 (West Supp. 1984).

the test materials,[27] forms,[28] or criteria for collection of specimens and interpretation of tests,[29] performing proficiency[30] or quality control[31] tests, establishing criteria regarding laboratory personnel,[32] having a physician convey the screening results to the child's physician or clinic,[33] specifying the type of test to be used,[34] requiring a minimum number of tests to be run per week,[35] or requiring the adoption of certain laboratory standards.[36] The Georgia statute provides for the development of a statewide network for medical genetics responsible for the training of personnel in genetics and quality control of laboratory services.[37]

Responsible Individual

The laws vary considerably regarding who has responsibility for assuring that a sample is obtained. In 22 states,[38] by statute or regulation, the responsibility be-

27. **Alaska** §18.15.200 (c) (1981); **Alaska** Admin. Code tit. 7 §27.540; **Me.** Dept. of Human Services, "Rules and Regulations Relating to Testing Newborn Infants for Detection of Causes of Mental Retardation" §6; **Md.** Admin. Code §10.38.07 (B) (1975); 7 **Minn.** Code Agency R. 1.172 C 2(a); **Or.** Admin. R. 333-24-220 (1) (1983); **R.I.** Dept. of Health Rules for Phenylketonuria Testing §2 (September 8, 1964) (department will provide necessary materials on request); and **Utah** Department of Social Services Division of Health, "Rules and Regulations Pertaining to Testing of Newborn Infants for Phenylketonuria and Other Metabolic Diseases Which May Result in Mental Retardation or Brain Damage" §IIIC (1978).

28. **Alaska** §18.15.200 (c) (1981); **Alaska** Admin. Code tit. 7 §27.540 (1983); **Ark.** Bd. of Health, Rules and Regulations Pertaining to the Testing of Newborn Infants for Phenylketonuria and Hypothyroidism §3 (B) (July 13, 1984); **Cal.** Admin. Code tit. 17 R. 6505(a), (e) (f) (1980); **Fla.** Stat. Ann. §383.14 (2) (b) (West Supp. 1984); and **S.D.** Codified Laws Ann. §34-24-23 (1977).

29. See, e.g., **Cal.** Admin. Code tit. 17 R. 6502 (c) (1980) (The department is required to make available such criteria); **Hawaii** Dept. of Health Administrative Rules, ch. 142 §11-142-5 (d) (1981); and **Kansas** Bureau of Maternal and Child Health, "Re: Reporting of PKU Screening Results."

30. **Ind.** State Bd. of Health, "Newborn Screening Program for Phenylketonuria and Hypothyroidism: Guidelines" p. 5 (July 1982) (lists various proficiency testing programs in which laboratories may participate); **Mich.** Admin Code R. 325.1473 (c) (e) (1966); and **Mo.** Admin. Code tit. 13 §50-143.010 (4) (B) 1-6.

31. **Cal.** Health and Safety Code §309 (West Supp. 1984).

32. 5 **Colo.** Code Reg. 1005-4 (III) (1) (a) (c) (1977).

33. **Conn.** Dept. of Public Health Screening Guidelines.

34. See e.g., **Mo.** Admin. Code tit. 13, §50-143.010 (3) (B) (1981); **Okla.** Board of Health, "Rules and Regulations Specifying Approved Tests and Requirements for Approved Laboratories Performing Tests for Phenylketonuria"; **Or.** Admin. R. 333-24-230 (1983); 28 **Pa.** Admin. Code §28.3 (1980); and **S.C.** Metabolic Disorders Screening Program Rules and Regulations §C (1) (1980).

35. **Mo.** Admin. Code tit. 13 §150-143.010 (3) (B) (3) (1981).

36. **S.C.** Dept. of Health and Environment Control, Metabolic Disorders Screening Program Rules and Regulations §C (2) (1980).

37. **Ga.** Code Ann. §31-12-5 (a), (b) (Supp. 1984).

38. **Ala.** Code 22-20-3 (a) (Supp. 1982); **Colo.** Rev. Stat. §25-4-802 (1) (1982); **Conn.** Gen. Stat. Ann. §19a-55 (a) (West Supp. 1982); **D.C.** Code Ann. §6-313 (a) (1981); **Idaho** Code §39-909 (1977); **Ind.** Code Ann. §16-8-6-6 (b) (Burns 1983); **Kan.** Stat. Ann. §65-181 (1980); **Ky.** Rev. Stat. §214.155 (1) (1982); 902 **Ky.** Admin. Regs. 4:1030(1); **Me.** Rev. Stat. Ann. tit. 22, §1522 (1980) (the statute provides that the department may authorize the hospital to be responsible; the regulations do so); **Me.** Dept. of Human Services, "Rules and Regulations Relating to Testing Newborn Infants for Detection of Causes of Mental Retardation" §1; **Md.** Admin. Code §10.38.04 (1975); **Minn.** Stat. Ann. §144.125 (West Supp. 1983); **Mont.** Code Ann. §50-19-203 (1) (1983); **Nev.** Rev. Stat. §442.115 (2) (1979); **N.H.** Rev. Stat. Ann. §132:10-a (1978); **N.M.** Stat. Ann. §24-1-6 (D) (Supp. 1982); **N.Y.** Pub. Health Law §2500-a (a) (McKinney 1972); **Or.** Admin. R. 333-24-215 (1) (a) (1983); **Pa.** Stat. Ann. tit. 35, §621 (Purdon 1977); **Pa.** 28 Admin. Code §28.21 (1980); Rules of **Tenn.** Dept. of Public Health Bureau of Community Health Services Administration §1200-15-1-.02 (1) (a) (1982); **Utah** Department of Social Services Division of Health, "Rules and Regulations Pertaining to Testing of Newborn Infants for Phenylketonuria and Other Metabolic Diseases which may Result in Mental Retardation or Brain Damage §III (A) and (B) (1978); and **Wash.** Admin. Code R 248-102-020 (1980). In Illinois, the physician is responsible but he or she may sometimes delegate that responsibility to the hospital administrator. **Ill.** Admin. Reg. §661.2 (1981).

longs to the health care institution or its chief administrative officer.[39] In 4 states,[40] only the health care facility or administrator is responsible. In other states, that responsibility is shared with others--most often the physician or birth attendant,[41] the person required to register the birth[42] or both[43]. Oregon specifies the order of responsibility; it lies first with the hospital or health care facility, second with the physician and, if no physician is in attendance, third with the parent or legal guardian.[44] In Arizona, although the birth attendant has responsibility to order the test, the person in charge of the institution must assure that the records show that the test was done or the parents refused.[45]

In 32 states, the physician or other birth attendant has responsibility for assuring that a sample is obtained.[46] Although most of the statutes appear to have been written to deal with in-hospital births, presumably the physician or birth attendant would similarly have responsibility with respect to an out-of-hospital birth. In those states which make the health care facility or administrator solely responsible, there is no provision for handling out-of-hospital births; the same is true in Wisconsin where the statute puts the responsibility on the attending physician for each infant born in a hospital or maternity home but gives no guidance for other births.

39. In an additional state, South Carolina, according to the Official Departmental Instructions of the South Carolina Department of Health and Environmental Control, hospital personnel have responsibility only if there is no attending physician.

40. **Conn.** Gen. Stat. Ann. §19a-55 (a) (West Supp. 1984); **D.C.** Code Ann. §6-313 (a) (1981); **Mont.** Code Ann. §50-19-203 (1) (1983); and **Wash.** Admin. Code R 248-102-020 (1980). In Maryland, the person in charge of the birth facility has sole responsibility for in-hospital births. **Md.** Admin. Code §10.38.04 (A) (1975).

41. See, e.g., the statutes of Alabama, Indiana, Kansas, Maine, New Hampshire, Nevada, New Mexico, Pennsylvania and Tennessee cited in n. 38.

42. See, e.g., the statutes of Idaho, Kentucky, Minnesota, and New York cited in n. 38.

43. See, e.g., the regulation of Utah (for out-of-hospital births) cited in n. 38.

44. **Or.** Admin. R. 333-24-215 (1) (a) (1983).

45. **Ariz.** Admin. Comp. R9-14-514 (2) (1979).

46. **Ala.** Code 22-20-3 (a) (1984) (under the regulations, this responsibility may be delegated to the appropriate nursery, laboratory, or office staff. **Alaska** Admin. Code tit. 7 §27.520 (1983)); **Alaska** Stat. §18.15.200 (a) (1981); **Ariz.** Rev. Stat. Ann. §36-694 (B) (Supp. 1983); **Cal.** Admin. Code tit. 17, R. 6505 (i); **Colo.** Rev. Stat. §25-4-1004 (1) (for a birth outside of a hospital); **Fla.** Admin. Code §10D-76.03 (5) (1978); **Ga.** Admin. Comp. ch. 290-5-24.02(2) (1983); **Hawaii** Rev. Stat. Part I §333-1 (1984); **Ill.** Admin. Reg. §661.2 (1981); **Ind.** Code Ann. §16-8-6-6 (b) (Burns 1983); **Iowa** Admin. Code §470-4.2 (136A); **Kan.** Stat. Ann. §65-181 (1980); **La.** Rev. Stat. Ann. §40.1299.1 (West Supp. 1984); Maine regs §1 (regulation); **Mass.** Ann. Laws ch 111, §110A (Michie/Law Co-op. Supp. 1983); **Mich.** Comp. Laws Ann. §333.5431 (1) (West 1980); **Minn.** Code Agengy R. §1.172 (B) (4) (1979); **Miss.** Code Ann. §41-21-203 (1981); **Nev.** Rev. Stat. §442.115 (2) (1979); **N.H.** Rev. Stat. Ann. §132:10-a (1978); **N.M.** Regs §203 (if child not born in hospital); **N.D.** Cent. Code §25-17-04 (1978); **Pa.** Stat. Ann. tit 35, §621 (Purdon 1977); **Pa.** Code ch. 28, §28.21 (1980); **R.I.** Gen. Laws §23-13-12 (1976); **South Carolina** Department of Health and Environmental Control Official Departmental Instructions §D; Rules of **Tenn.** Dept. of Public Health Bureau of Community Health Services Administration §1200-15-1-.02 (1) (a) (1982); **Tx.** Rev. Civ. Stat. Ann. art. 4447e §2, art. 4447e-1 §3 (Vernon Supp. 1984); **Utah** Regs. §IIIA, §IIIB (1978); **Va.** Code §32.1-65 (Supp. 1984); **W. Va.** Code §16-22-3 (Supp. 1983); **Wis.** Stat. Ann. §146.02(1) (West Supp. 1982-1983); and **Wyo.** Regs, ch. 35, §4 (B) (only if born outside of hospital). Some of these statutes cover all health care professionals who might deliver a child. Hawaii, for example, makes the physician, midwife or birth attendant responsible. **Hawaii** Rev. Stat. part I §333-1 (1984). Other statutes, such as Rhode Island's, just specify the physician, which leads to the possibility that an infant delivered by someone else might not be screened. **R.I.** Gen. Laws §23-13-12 (1976). In Indiana, the responsibility of the hospital and physician includes not only assuring that the sample is obtained, but also causing that sample to be transported to a designated laboratory. **Ind.** Code Ann. §16-8-6-6 (b) (Burns 1983).

A few states directly address the issue of who is responsible when an out-of-hospital birth occurs--either targeting the physician or birth attendant,[47] the person who registers the birth,[48] the nurse who first visits the child,[49] the local public health nurse,[50] or the physician who first attends the child.[51] In Colorado, both the birth attendant and the person registering the birth have responsibility.[52]

In eight states,[53] the person registering the birth is among those with responsibility for taking a sample or otherwise assuring that one is obtained. In one other state, he or she has sole responsibility.[54]

The infants' parents are among those with responsibility for assuring that a sample is obtained in 2 states.[55] In Missouri, the parents have sole responsibility for assuring that screening is done.[56] However, the Missouri regulations give the attending physician or other health professional the duty of notifying parents of their responsibility to have testing performed.[57]

Rescreening and Verifying Testing

A minority of states recommend or require mandatory rescreening of newborns.[58] Other states have enacted mechanisms to check if the initial screening occurred.

47. See, e.g., **Cal.** Admin. Code tit. 17, R 6505 (j); **Fla.** Admin. Code §10-D-76.03 (6) (1978); **Ga.** Admin. Comp. ch. 290-5-24.02 (6) (1983); and **N.M.** Reg. §203 (1979). In Wyoming, the statute is silent on who is responsible for screening and the regulation covers only births outside of health care facilities. **Wyo.** Reg. §4(b).

48. See, e.g., **Md.** Admin. Code §10.38.05 (1975); **Mont.** Admin. Code 16-2.18 (6)-51820 (8), **N.Y.** Admin. Code tit. 10, §69.2(d) (1978). In Iowa, the person who registers the birth has the responsibility for informing the parents that they should have the test done. **Iowa** Admin. Code §470-4.4 (136A)

49. **Alaska** Stat. §18.15.200(a) (1981).

50. **N.H.** Dept. of Health and Welfare Div. of Public Health Services, Bureau for the Handicapped Children, "Recommendations for Newborn Specimen Screening Collection" 1(F) (March 18, 1983) (if there is no physician, the family should be advised to contact their local public health nurse).

51. **Ill.** Admin. Reg. §661.2 (1981), **Va.** Code §32.1-65 (Supp. 1984).

52. **Colo.** Rev. Stat. §25-4-1004 (1) and -802 (1) (1983).

53. **Ariz.** Rev. Stat. Ann. §36-694B (Supp. 1983); **Colo.** Rev. Stat. §25-4-802 (1) (1982) (if child not born in institution or not tested, the person responsible for signing the birth certificate); **Idaho** Code §39-909 (1977); **Ky.** Stat. §214.155 (1) (1982); 902 **Ky.** Admin. Regs. §4:030 (1). **Md.** Admin. Code §10.38.05 (1975) (by regulation for an out-of-health care facility birth); **Minn.** Stat. Ann. §144.125 (West Supp. 1983); **N.Y.** Pub. Health Law §2500-a (a) (McKinney 1972); and **N.Y.** Admin. Code tit. 10, §69.2 (d) (1978) (if child born outside institution). **Utah** Department of Social Services Division of Health, "Rules and Regulations Pertaining to Testing of Newborn Infants for Phenylketonuria and Other Metabolic Diseases which may result in Mental Retardation or Brain Damage" §III (A) and (B) (1978). In Iowa, the person registering an out-of-health facility birth must inform the parents of the availability of screening. **Iowa** Admin. Code §470-4.4 (136A).

54. **Ohio** Rev. Code Ann. §3701.501 (A) (Baldwin 1984).

55. Illinois (by regulation, if there is no attending physician) **Ill.** Admin. Reg. §661.2 (1981), **S.C.** Dept. of Health and Environmental Control, "Metabolic Disorders Screening Program Rules and Regulations" (by departmental instruction if there is no physician) **S.C.** §D. (1980).

56. **Mo.** Ann. Stat. §210.065.1 (Vernon 1983).

57. **Mo.** Admin. Code, tit. 13 §50-143.010 (1) (B) (1981).

58. See, e.g., **Md.** Admin. Code §10.38.06 (1975) (strongly recommends second test on the child's first visit to the doctor, preferably when the child is between the ages of one and four weeks); **N.H.** Dept. of Health and Welfare Division of Public Health Services Bureau for Handicapped Children, "Recommendations for Newborn Screening Specimen Collection" (recommends routine

The California regulations require that the hospital review each newborn's medical record within 14 days from discharge to determine that the tests were done and the results recorded.[59] The South Carolina regulations mandate a similar review by the hospital no later than ten days after delivery to ensure the specimen was collected and submitted.[60] In South Dakota, the Department of Health receives tests results on all children screened to match against birth certificates.[61] The Washington regulations provide the possibility for a similar check by requiring weekly reporting of all live births in the genetics program.[62]

Some states try to assure that children who do inadvertently slip through the screening system are nonetheless diagnosed. In Pennsylvania, for example, the regulations provide that if a child exhibits signs suggestive of metabolic disease and has not already been determined to be affected, the health care facility or practitioner shall collect a blood specimen for metabolic disease testing.[63]

Program Procedures

The issues of the timing and the manner of screening and the type of test to be used for screening is specified in the statutes of very few states. Generally, the responsibility for making determinations about how testing is to be undertaken is delegated to some administrative agency such as the department of health. Similarly, the statutes rarely specify the procedures for confirmatory testing or follow-up.

The issue of treatment is addressed in few states. Some statutes provide that rules should be promulgated for treatment,[64] and a few states have done so.[65]

---

rescreening if the infant is discharged prior to 48 hours of life); **N.M.** Health and Environment Dept., "Newborn Screening Program Regulation" §206 (July 1, 1979) (mandatory PKU rescreening before the child is two weeks old); **Tx.** Dept. of Health, Maternal and Child Health Services, 'Testing Newborn Children for Phenylketonuria, Other Hereditable Diseases and Hypothyroidism" §37.55(a) (1983) (mandatory PKU retesting of all infants discharged prior to 24 hours after protein feeding was started); Rules of **Tenn.** Dept. of Public Health Bureau of Community Health Services Administration §1200-15-1-.02 (1) (b) (1982) (rescreen at two weeks if infant is screened earlier than 48 hours after birth); **Utah** Department of Social Services Division of Health, "Rules and Regulations Pertaining to Testing of Newborn Infants for Phenylketonuria and Other Metabolic Diseases Which May Result in Mental Retardation or Brain Damage" §III (E) (1978) (mandatory rescreening when the infant is two to four weeks old); and **Wyo.** Dept. of Health and Social Services, "Mandatory Screening of Newborn Infants for Inborn Errors of Metabolism," ch. 35 §5 (mandatory PKU rescreening when the infant is two weeks old).

59. **Cal.** Admin. Code tit. 17 R. 6505 (d) (1980).

60. **S.C.** Metabolic Disorders Screening Program Rules and Regulations §D (2) (e) (1980).

61. Letter from Allen W. Krom, Health Services Assistant Administrator, Maternal and Child Health Program, South Dakota Department of Health, Division of Health Services, June 20, 1983.

62. **Wash.** Admin. Code R. 248-29-050 (11) (b) (1980).

63. 28 **Pa.** Admin. Code §28.28 (1980).

64. **Ala.** Code §22-20-3 (b) (1984); **Ga.** Code Ann. §31-12-6 (a) (Supp. 1984); **N.J.** Stat. Ann. §26:5B-4b (West Supp. 1982-83); and **Va.** Code §32.1-67 (Supp. 1984).

65. See, e.g., **Va.** Bd. of Health, "Rules and Regulations . . . Governing Detection and Control of Phenylketonuria" §§4.03, 5.01 (April 1, 1982).

Other statutes provide that the department shall provide services for treatment of any diagnosed case,[66] assist in treatment and care of affected infants,[67] or actually provide the treatment.[68] In some states, the type of therapy that should be instituted after diagnosis is specified in the regulations.[69] Other statutes provide a means for obtaining a consultant[70] or for designating a physician to help the parent and her physician secure appropriate follow-up, testing and treatment.[71] In Ohio, the Director of Health is required to assist in developing treatment programs and providing for habilitation.[72] Often, the issue of treatment is addressed more fully in statutes other than the newborn screening statutes, such as a Crippled Children's Act or a Genetically Handicapped Person's Program.[73] Assessment of the care of affected children is rarely addressed in the newborn screening laws or regulations. The Louisiana guidelines are an exception. They provide for monitoring plasma levels in phenylketonuria patients[74] and provide that a phenylketonuria child "should be evaluated at regular intervals as recommended by the attending physician or the consultant psychologist."[75]

Time Constraints

Some states try to assure that infants are screened, diagnosed and treated in a timely manner by specifying the time period by which samples must be sent to the

66. **Alaska** §18.15.200 (d) (1981); **Idaho** Code §39-910 (5) (1977) (the director will supervise local health agencies in treatment and cure of affected individuals); **Ill.** Ann. Stat. ch. 111½ §4904 (d) (Smith-Hurd 1983) (the department will arrange for or provide public health nursing, nutrition and social services and clinical consultation as indicated); **N.D.** State Dept. of Health Div. of Maternal and Child Health, "Newborn Metabolic Screening Policy Statement" (November 1982) (provides for various follow-up services including assistance with dietary management, in-home follow-up, and special formulae free of charge to the needy); 28 **Pa.** Admin. Code §28.30 (b) (1980) (the department will arrange for referral, diagnosis, treatment, habilitative and other follow-up services); **Tx.** Rev. Civ. Stat. Ann. art. 4447e §2 (Vernon Supp. 1984) and 4447e-1 §7 (Vernon Supp. 1984); and **Wash.** Rev. Code Ann. §70.83.040 (West Supp. 1982).

67. **Ark.** Stat. Ann. §82-626 (6) (Supp. 1983).

68. **Fla.** Stat. Ann. §383.14 (2) (e) (West Supp. 1984) (where practicable when the products are not otherwise available); **Ga.** Code Ann. §31-12-7 (b) (Supp. 1984) (treatment for phenylketonuria and sickle cell anemia is available without cost); **Ill.** Ann. Stat. ch. 111½, §4904 (c) (Smith-Hurd 1983) (where practicable when treatment product not available through other state agencies); **Kan.** Stat. Ann. §65-180 (d) (1980) (the secretary will provide the necessary treatment when the product is not available through other state agencies); **La.** Rev. Stat. Ann. §40.1299.1 (West Supp. 1984); **La.** Dept. of Health and Human Resources, "Guidelines: Neonatal Screening Programs" §IIIB, E; **N.D.** Cent. Code §25-17-03 (2) (1978) (the Department will make arrangements for treatment where indicated and the family is unable to pay); and **Va.** Code §32.1-67 (Supp. 1984) (for medically indigent families).

69. **Ark.** Bd. of Health, Rules and Regulations Pertaining to the Testing of Newborn Infants for Phenylketonuria and Hypothyroidism §7 (C), (D) (July 13, 1984); and **Ill.** Admin. Reg. §661.6 (1981).

70. **Ark.** Bd. of Health, Rules and Regulations Pertaining to the Testing of Newborn Infants for Phenylketonuria and Hypothyroidism §7 (A) (July 13, 1984); **Fla.** Dept. of Health and Rehabilitative Services, "Guidelines for the Florida Infant Screening Program" (April 1981); **Ill.** Admin. Reg. §661.6 (1981); Indiana State Board of Health, "Newborn Screening Program for Phenylketonuria and Hypothyroidism: Guidelines" 4 (July 1982); 28 **Pa.** Admin. Code §§28.30 (b), 28.31 (b) (1980); and **Va.** Bd. of Health "Rules and Regulations . . . Governing the Detection and Control of Phenylketonuria" §5.01 (April 1, 1982).

71. **D.C.** Code Ann. §6-313(c) (1981).

72. **Ohio** Rev. Code Ann. §3701.502 (A) (Baldwin 1984).

73. **Cal.** Health and Safety Code §340-348 (West Supp. 1984).

74. **La.** Dept. of Health and Human Resources, "Guidelines: Neonatal Screening Programs" §III C(3).

75. **La.** Dept. of Health and Human Resources, "Guidelines: Neonatal Screening Programs" §III E(5).

laboratory (ranging from the same day to within 72 hours),[76] that samples must be analyzed (generally ranging from three to ten days),[77] that laboratories must report (ranging from one day to two weeks)[78] or that a final diagnosis must be made (for example, 14 days).[79] Other states set a time limit during which the entire process must take place. In Indiana, "the screening test and all follow-up confirmatory and diagnostic studies must be accomplished early enough so that therapy, when indicated, can be initiated no later than 21 days of age."[80]

Reporting Procedures

The statutes and regulations require reporting of results to one or more of the following individuals and entities: the physician (25 states),[81] the hospital (11

76. See, e.g., **Conn.** Agencies Regs. §19-13-D41(C) (1979) (specimens must be sent to laboratory within forty-eight hours after collection); **Me.** Dept. of Human Services, "Rules and Regulations Relating to Testing Newborn Infants for Detection of Causes of Mental Retardation: §6 (requires that specimens be shipped daily to the Department of Human Services, Public Health Laboratory); **Md.** Admin. Code §10.38.07(c) (1975) (sample must be mailed to the laboratory within 24 hours of collection); **Mo.** Admin. Code tit. 13 §50-143.010(3)(A)(4) (1981) (blood samples must be submitted to the laboratory no later than 72 hours after collection); **N.M.** Health and Environment Dept., "Newborn Screening Program Regulations" §204 (July 1, 1979) (specimen must be sent for testing within 24 hours of its collection); **Ohio** Admin. Code §3701-45-01(D)(4) (1981) (specimens must be sent to the laboratory no later than 48 hours after collection); **Or.** Admin. R. 333-24-220(2) (1983) (samples must be sent to the lab within 24 hours after collection); **Pa.** Admin. Code §28.4 (1980) (specimens must be submitted within 48 hours of collection); **S.C.** Metabolic Disorders Screening Program Official Departmental Instructions (1980) (the attending physician is responsible for collecting the sample and sending it to the laboratory that same day); and **Wash.** Admin. Code R. 248-102-020(1) (1980) (the sample must be sent by the next working day after collection to the Health Services Division Laboratory).

77. See, e.g., **Ark.** State Bd. of Health, "Rules and Regulations Pertaining to the Testing of Newborn Infants for Phenylketonuria and Hypothyroidism," §3(B) (July 13, 1984) (analysis must be done within a time period which would allow preventive medical intervention 5 **Colo.** Code Reg. 1005-4 (III) (3) (1977)) (tests must be performed by the laboratory within a week); **Ill.** Admin. Reg. §661.3(e) (1981) (all tests shall be performed within 10 days of collection of the blood sample); **Mich.** Admin. Code R. 325.1473(d) (1966) (tests must be performed no later than three days after receipt of specimen); and **Ohio** Admin. Code §3701-45-01(B)(1) (1981) (tests must be completed within three working days of submission).

78. **Conn.** Agencies Reg. §19-13-D41(f) (1979) (results of tests must be reported to the state department of health within 24 hours); **Fla.** Admin. Code §10D-76.06(1) (the laboratory must report results within 7-10 days after receipt of the sample); **Iowa** Admin. Code §470-4.5(1) (136A) (the laboratory shall test samples within 24 hours of receipt); **Md.** Admin. Code §10.38.09(A) (1975) (the laboratory must notify the Department of any abnormal results within a week of receipt of the specimen); **Mont.** Admin. Code 16-2.18(6)-S1820(3) (the laboratory must report all positive or suspicious test results to the Department within 48 hours after drawing the blood and performing the test); and **N.C.** Division of Health Services of the Department of Human Resources, "PKU and Hypothyroidism Protocol" §II (I) (the maximum turnaround time from receipt of the specimen to notification of the physician shall not exceed two weeks).

79. According to the **Utah** regulations, when an infant with a positive of questionable screening test result is referred to a physician for quantitative evaluation, the physician must make the final diagnosis and notify the Division of Health within 14 days. **Utah** Department of Social Services State Division of Health has adopted "Rules and Regulations Pertaining to Testing of Newborn Infants for Phenylketonuria and Other Metabolic Diseases Which May Result in Mental Retardation or Brain Damage" §IV(E) (1978).

80. **Ind.** State Bd. of Health, "Newborn Screening Program for Phenylketonuria: Guidelines" p. 3 (July 1982). See also **Ga.** Code Ann. §31-12-6(b) (1982) (the entire process for screening, retrieval and diagnosis must occur within the first three weeks of an infant's life).

81. **Alaska** Stat. §18.15.200 (d) (1981) (confirmed phenylketonuria cases); **Alaska** Admin. Code tit. 7 §27.550(c) (1983) (positive or abnormal results); 5 **Colo.** Code Rg. 1005-4 (III-4) (1977) **Connecticut** Department of Health Services Guidelines (physician in Maternal and Child Health Section reports abnormal results to attending physician); **Fla.** Admin. Code §10D-76.06 (1) (1978); **Ga.** Admin. Comp. ch. 290-5-24.02 (7) and (8) (1983); **Hawaii** Dept. of Health Administrative Rules, ch. 142 §11-142-3 (c) (2) (1981) (presumptive positives); **Idaho** regs. §2-12105.02 (b) (1980); **Iowa** Admin. Code §470-4.5 (2) (136A) (presumptive positives); 902 **Ky.** Admin. Regs. §4:030 (2) (positives); **Me.** Dept. of Human Services, "Rules and Regulations Relating to Testing Newborn Infants for Detection of Causes of Mental Retardation" §6; **Md.** Admin. Code §10.38.07 (D) (1975); **Mich.** Admin. Code R. 325.1473 (f) (1966) (presumptive positives); 7 **Minn.** Code Agency R. §1.172 (C) 2 (c) (1979) (positives); **Mo.** Admin. Code tit. 13 §50-143.010 (5) (1981); **N. H.** Dept. of Health and Welfare Division of Public Health Services Bureau for the Handicapped Children, "Recommendations for Newborn Screening Specimen Collection (March 18, 1983) (positive results reported directly to physician; hospital also place copy of test results in physician's box) (recommendation); **N. M.** Health and Environment Dept. "Newborn Screening Program Recommendations" §207 (positive or questionable results); **N.C.** Protocol I, II (protocol); **N.D.** Policy Statement p. 6 (positives); **Pa.** Admin. Code, ch. 28, §28.24 (b) (1980); **S.C.** Dept. of Health and Environmental

states),[82] the family (12 states),[83] the department (26 states),[84] a designated physician (1 jurisdiction),[85] or the submittor of the test (2 states).[86] The regulations include further details about the timing and mode of communication of the test results. In 10 states, however, the reporting procedures are not specified by either the statutes or the regulations.[87] In some states, physicians are additionally required to report cases of affected individuals.[88] In Michigan, there is an apparent conflict

---

Control, "Metabolic Disorders Screening Program Rules and Regulations" §E (1) (1980); **Va.** Code §32.1-69 (1982); **Wash.** Admin. Code §248-102-040 (2) (3) (for presumptive positive, the laboratory notifies the physician or family); **Wis.** Stat. Ann. §146.02 (4) (West Supp. 1982-1983); and **Wyo.** Dept. of Health and Social Services, "Mandatory Screening of Newborn Infants for Inborn Errors of Metabolism," ch. 35, §5 (positive or questionable results). The Indiana guidelines provide a sample form for reporting results to physicians. **Indiana** State Board of Health, "Newborn Screening Program for Phenylktonuria and Hypothyroidism: Guidelines" 11 (July 1982).

82. 5 **Colo.** Code Reg. §1005-4 (III) (4) (1977); **D.C.** Code Ann. §6-313 (c) (1981); **Fla.** Admin. Code §10D-76.06 (1) (1978); **Ga.** Admin. Comp. ch. 290-5-24.02 (7) and (8) (1983) (additionally, if the results are abnormal, the facility calls the physician or, if he or she is unavailable, the parents); **Idaho** tit. 2, ch. 12, "Rules Governing Procedures and Testing to be Performed on Newborn Infants" 2-12105.02 (b) (1980); **Iowa** Admin. Code §470.4.5 (2) (136A) (presumptive positives); **Me.** Dept. of Human Services, "Rules and Regulations Relating to Testing Newborn Infants for Detection of Causes of Mental Retardation" §6; **Md.** Admin. Code §10.38.07 (D) (1975); **N. H.** Dept. of Health and Welfare Division of Public Health Services Bureau for the Handicapped Children "Recommendations for Newborn Screening Specimen Collection" (1983); **N.C.** Protocol I, II (protocol); and **Pa.** Admin. Code, ch. 28, §28.24 (b) (1980).

83. **Colo.** Rev. Stat. §25-4-1004 (1) (1983) (physician to tell parent); **D.C.** Code Ann. §6-313 (c) (1981) (positives); **Fla.** Admin. Code §10D-76.06 (3) (c) (1978) (positive) (physician or county health unit shall report abnormal results to parent); **Md.** Pub. Health Code Ann. §13-109 (e) (3) (1982) (unambiguous results are available to family through physician or other source of health care); **Mich.** Comp. Laws Ann. §333.5431 (1) (West 1980) (positive); **N.D.** Policy Statement (positives); **Pa.** Code, ch. 28, §28.27 (1980) (presumptive positives are reported to family by physician or health care facility); **S.C.** Dept. of Health and Environmental Control, "Metabolic Disorders Screening Program Rules and Regulations" 13B, §E (1980) (physician tells parents); **Va.** Code §32.1-69 (1982); **Wash.** Admin. Code §248-102-040 (2) (3) (for presumptive positive, the laboratory notifies physician or family); and **Wis.** Stat. Ann. §146.02 (4) (West Supp. 1982-1983) (physician to tell parents). The Indiana guidelines have a sample form for reporting to parents. **Indiana** State Board of Health, "Newborn Screening Program for Phenylketonuria and Hypothyroidism: Guidelines" 10 (July 1982).

84. **Alaska** Stat. §18.15.200 (d) (confirmed phenylketonuria diagnosis); **Ark.** Stat. Ann. §§82.625, 82-626 (6) (Supp. 1983) (positives); 5 **Colo.** Code Reg. §1005-4 (III) (4) (positives) (1977); **Conn.** Agencies Regs. §19-13-D 41 (f) (1979) (abnormal results must be communicated to the Maternal and Child Health Section); **Fla.** Admin. Code §10D-76.06 (3) (a) (1978) (positives); **Ga.** Admin. Comp. ch. 290-5-24.02 (7) (1983) (sickle cell anemia results are reported to county health department); **Ill.** Admin. Reg. §661.5 (b) (1981) (hospitals performing screening shall immediately report abnormal results to the Department of Public Health); **Iowa** Admin. Code §470-4.5 (4) (periodic reports to the Birth Defects Institute); §470-4.5 (2) (presumptive positives reported to Birth Defects Institute); **Ky.** Rev. Stat. §214.155 (1) (1982) (positives); 902 **Ky.** Admin. Regs. §4:030 (2) (positives); **La.** Rev. Stat. Ann. §40.1299.1 (West Supp. 1984) (physician notifies department of positives); **Me.** Rev. Stat. Ann. tit. 22, §1522 (1980) (reports may be required to be submitted to the department); **Md.** Admin. Code §10.38.09 (A) (1975) (positives) §10.38.07 (D) (1975) (local health department gets all results); **Mich.** Admin. Code R. §325-1473(F) (1966) (presumptive positives); **Mo.** Admin. Code tit. 13 §50-143.010 (5); **Mont.** Admin. Code 16-2.18 (6) - S1820 (3); **Neb.** Rev. Stat. §71-604.04 (1981); **Nev.** Rev. Stat. §442.115 (3) (a) (1979) (positives reported to local health officer); **N. M.** Health and Environment Dept. "Newborn Screening Program Recommendations" §207 (July 1, 1979) (positive or questionable results); **N.C.** Protocol I, II (protocol); **N.D.** Policy Statement (physician attending case must report the case to the State Department of Public Health unless the parents object on religious grounds); **Okla.** Bd. of Health "Rules and Regulations Specifying Approved Tests and Requirements for Approved Laboratories Performing Tests for Phenylketonuria" (1971) (presumptive positives); **Pa.** Code, ch. 28, §28.27 (1980) (presumptive positives reported to the department if child's parents can't be notified within 48 hours); **S.D.** Codified Laws Ann. §34-24-23 (1977); **Wash.** Rev. Code Ann. §70.83.030 (West Supp. 1982) (positives); **W. Va.** Code §16-22-3 (Supp. 1983) (positives); and **Wyo.** Dept. of Health and Social Services, "Mandatory Screening of Newborn Infants for Inborn Errors of Metabolism" ch. 35, §5 (positive or questionable test results).

85. **D.C.** Code Ann. §6-313 (c) (1981) (positive results).

86. **Arkansas** State Board of Health, "Rules and Regulations Pertaining to the Testing of Newborn Infants for Phenylketonuria and Hypothyroidism" §§5 (A), 6 (A) (2) (July 13, 1984); **Texas** Dept. of Health Maternal and Child Health Services "Testing Newborn Children for Phenylketonuria, Other Heritable Diseases, and Hypothyroidism" §37.55 (1983).

87. See, e.g., Alabama; Arizona; Massachusetts; New Jersey; New York (the statute provides that reporting shall be done in the manner prescribed by the Commissioner); Ohio; Rhode Island; Tennessee (the statute provides that regulation shall be adopted in this issue); and Utah (the statute provides that regulation shall be adopted in this issue). In Montana, the statute authorizes the adoption of regulations requiring reporting to the physician or family, but the regulations merely specify that reports of all positives or suspicious results be reported to the department. **Mont.** Admin. Code 16-2.18 (6) -S1820 (3).

88. See, e.g., **Cal.** Admin. Code tit. 17, R. 6505 (r); **Kan.** Stat. Ann. §65-183 (1980); **Mo.** Ann. Stat. §210.065.2 (Vernon 1983); 7 **Minn.** Code Agency R. §1.172(C) (1979) (mandating that the physician notify the Human Genetics Unit of confirmed cases); **N.D.** Cent. Code §25-17-04 (1978); **Ore.** Rev. Stat. §433.295 (1) (1981); **Va.** and Code §32.1-66 (1982).

between the statute and the regulations. The statute requires reporting to the parents or guardian,[89] while the regulations require reporting to the physician and the state health director.[90]

Recordkeeping

The recording of results is not covered under the majority of the laws and regulations. No state statute provides guidelines for recording. In 8 states, the statutes mandate the adoption of regulations to cover recordkeeping, but such regulations apparently have not been adopted.[91] Fourteen other states have adopted regulations or guidelines to cover recording, however.[92] In some states, the time period for which records must be kept is specified--21 years in Ohio,[93] 5 years in Connecticut,[94] and 3 years in Florida.[95] Under the Louisiana guidelines, the central laboratory must maintain a permanent record of all positive tests.[96]

Registries and Confidentiality

Nine states by statute and three others by regulations or guidelines establish registries.[97] In six of these states,[98] there are special provisions to assure the infor-

89. **Mich.** Comp. Laws Ann. §333.5431 (1) (West 1980).

90. **Mich.** Admin. Code R. 325.1473(f).

91. **Ala.** Code §22-20-3 (a) (1984); **Colo.** Rev. Stat. §25-4-1003 (1) (e) (1983); **Kan.** Stat. Ann. §65-181 (1980); **Ky.** Rev. Stat. §214.155 (1) (1982); **Md.** Pub. Health Code Ann. §13-108 (2) (1982); and **S.C.** Code Ann. §44-37-30 (Law Co-op. Supp. 1983). In Maine, the statute authorizes adoption of a regulation requiring records to be submitted to the department. **Me.** Rev. Stat. Ann. tit. 22, §1522 (1980). In Nebraska, the Director of Health may require test results be recorded on the birth certificate. **Neb.** Rev. Stat. §71-604.01 (3) (1981).

92. **Ark.** State Bd. of Health, "Rules and Regulations Pertaining to the Testing of Newborn Infants for Phenylketonuria and Hypothyroidism" §3B (1984); **Cal.** Admin. Code tit. 17, R. 6504 (a) and (b); **Conn.** Agencies Reg. §19-13-D41(g) (1979); **Fla.** Admin. Code §§10D - 76.07 (1), - (3) (1978); April 1981 Guidelines VII (c); **Ga.** Admin. Comp. ch. §290-5-24.02 (7) (1983); **Hawaii** Dept. of Health Administrative Rules, ch. 142 §11-142-3 (a) (1981); **Idaho** tit. 2, ch. 12, "Rules Governing Procedures and Testing to be Performed on Newborn Infants" §§2-12105.02 (d), .03 (f) (1980); **Ind.** State Board of Health Screening Guidelines, p. 3; **La.** Guidelines §III C (1) (b); 7 **Minn.** Code Agency R. §1.127 C (1) (c) (2) (b) (1979); **Mont.** Admin. Code 16-2.18 (6) - S1820 (9), (10) (d); **N. H.**, Dept. of Health and Welfare Div. of Public Health Services, Bureau for the Handicapped Children, "Recommendations for Newborn Specimen Screening Collection;" **Ohio** Public Health Council §3701-45-01 (B) (3); and **Wash.** Admin. Code R. 248-29-070 (2) (b) (1980).

93. **Ohio** Admin. Code §3701-45-01 (B) (3) (1981).

94. **Conn.** Agencies Regs. §19-13-D41(g) (1979).

95. **Fla.** Admin. Code §10D - 76.07 (1) (or in accordance with department records management procedures).

96. **La.** "Guidelines: Neonatal Screening Programs" IIIc (1) (b).

97. The statutes are: **Alaska** Stat. §18.05.044 (1974) (voluntary); **Fla.** Stat. Ann. §383.14 (2) (d) (West Supp. 1984), **Fla.** Admin. Code §§10D-76.07(2), (April 1981) and Guidelines VII(B); **Idaho** Code §39-910 (5) (1977); **Ill.** Ann. Stat. ch. 111½, §4904 (b) (Smith-Hurd 1983) and **Ill.** Admin. Reg. §661.6 (1981); **Kan.** Stat. Ann. §65-180 (c) (1980); **Neb.** Rev. Stat. §71-646 (1981); **N.J.** Stat. Ann. §26:8-40.21 (West Supp. 1984-85); **N.Y.** Pub. Health Law §2733 (1) (McKinney 1972) (reporting of birth defects); and **N.D.** Cent Code §25-17-03 (3) (1978). In **Iowa**, the statute provides that the Birth Defects Institute may establish a registry. **Iowa** Code Ann. §136A.6 (West Supp. 1984-5). The regulations are: **La.** Guidelines §IIIF; **Md.** Admin. Code §10-38.11 (1975); and 7 **Minn.** Code Agency R. §1.172 c 2(b) (1979).

98. **Alaska** Stat. §18.05.046 (1974); **Fla.** Stat. Ann. §383.14 (2) (d) (West Supp. 1984); **Iowa** Code Ann. §136A.6 (West Supp. 1984-5); **Md.** Admin. Code §10-38-11 (1975); **Neb.** Rev. Stat. §71-648 (1), -(2) (1981); and **N.Y.** Pub. Health Law §2733 (2) (McKinney 1972).

mation in the registries is confidential. Beyond the provisions for confidentiality of registry information, eleven states have broader provisions for the confidentiality of information obtained in genetics programs.[99]

Most of the registries are apparently mandatory, but one allows a religious exception.[100] The Alaska statute is the only one that explicitly provides that the registry is voluntary. It provides that no person with an impairment or parent of such a person may be compelled to furnish or consent to furnishing information for the case registry. Moreover, the written consent of the individual or parent must be obtained before any private or governmental organization, institution, or individual may furnish information to the registry.

Counseling and Education

A minority of states, 13, have provisions for counseling.[101] The North Carolina law provides that counseling shall be done only by adequately trained and certified persons.[102]

The provisions in Colorado are the most detailed, describing the required content of the counseling. According to the Colorado statute, "[a]ll participants in programs on genetic counseling and education shall be informed of the nature of possible risks involved in participation in such a program or project, and shall be informed of the nature and cost of available therapies of maintenance programs for those affected by hereditary disorders, and shall be informed of the possible benefits and risks of such therapies and programs. . . ."[103] Nevertheless, the statute limits the responsibility of those providing counseling. No hospital or other health facility or any physician or other health professional is required to provide genetic counseling "beyond the

99. **Cal.** Admin. Code tit. 17, R. 6505 (g); **Colo.** Rev. Stat. §25-4-1003 (2) (e), -(f) (1983); **D.C.** Code Ann. §6-314 (D) (1981); **Ga.** Code Ann. §31-12-2 (a) (Supp. 1984); **Md.** Pub. Health Code Ann. §13-109(c) (1982); **Neb.** Rev. Stat. §71-648 (2) (1981) (for reports made by physician to department); **N.J.** Stat. Ann. §26:2-111 (West Supp. 1982-1983); **Va.** Code §32.1-69 (1982); **Wash.** Admin. Code R. 248-29-070 (1) (1980) (for birth center records); **Wis.** Stat. Ann. §146.02 (4) (West Supp. 1982-83); and **Wyo.** Dept. of Health and Social Services, Division Regulations.

100. **Neb.** Rev. Stat. §71-648 (1) (1981).

101. **Ala.** Code §22-10A-2 (b) (2) (1984); **Cal.** Health & Safety Code §309 (West Supp. 1984); **Colo.** Rev. Stat. §§25-4-1003 (1) (a), (b), and (d) (1983); **D.C.** Code Ann. §6-314 (3) (c) (1981) (does not cover genetic counseling per se, but provides that participants in metabolic disorders programs be informed of the nature of risks of participation, the nature and cost of available therapies or maintenance programs for those affected by metabolic disorders, and the possible benefits and risks of such therapies and programs); **Fla.** Stat. Ann. §383.14 (2) (f) (West Supp. 1984); **Ga.** Code Ann. §§31-12-5 (b), -7(b), -7(c) (1982); **Iowa** Code Ann. §136A.3 (7) (West Supp. 1984-1985); **Md.** Pub. Health Code Ann. §13-109(g) (2) (1982); **N.Y.** Pub. Health Law §2732 (d) (McKinney 1972); **N.C.** Gen. Stat. §143B-195 (1973); **Ohio** Rev. Code Ann. §3701.502 (A) (Baldwin 1984); and **Va.** Code §32.1-68 (1982) (education of affected individuals and post-screening counseling). Montana provides that the department may determine for advising the physician, parents, or legal guardian of the availability of counseling. **Mont.** Code Ann. §50-19-204(2) (1982). Under the Nebraska statute the department may conduct and support clinical counseling services in medical facilities. **Neb.** Rev. Stat. §71-647 (4) (1981). Additionally, under **Ill.** Ann. Stat. ch. 111½ §4904 (d) (Smith-Hurd 1983), the department shall arrange for social services and clinical consultations as indicated.

102. **N.C.** Gen. Stat. §143B-196 (1973).

103. **Colo.** Rev. Stat. §25-4-1003 (2) (g) (1983).

usual and customary and accepted practice nor shall any hospital or other health facility be held liable for not providing such genetic counseling."[104] The Maryland law specifies the approach that the counseling must take; it must be non-directive, emphasize informing the individual and not require restrictions on childbearing.[105]

More common are provisions for the education of the public in general (3 states),[106] the profession (2 states)[107] or both (18 states)[108] about the causes, diagnosis and treatment of inborn errors of metabolism. The North Carolina statute provides that no voluntary testing program shall begin earlier than 60 days after an adequate and effective educational program.[109] Two statutes provide for education without specifying who the target of the education should be.[110]

Costs

The costs for screening are mentioned in a minority of states. Three states provide explicitly by statute that there shall be no charge for the screening.[111] Additionally, the North Carolina statute establishes a pilot program for sickle cell anemia and related genetic disorders that furnishes testing and counseling without cost to persons requesting them.[112] Twelve states provide that a charge may be levied.[113]

104. **Colo.** Rev. Stat. §25-4-1003 (2) (h) (1983).

105. **Md.** Pub. Health Code Ann. §13-109 (g) (2) (1982).

106. **D.C.** Code Ann. §6-316 (1), -(2), -(3) (1981); **Fla.** Stat. Ann. §383.14 (2) (c) (West Supp. 1984); and **Md.** Pub. Health Code Ann. §13-108 (1) (1982).

107. **N.Y.** Pub. Health Law §2732 (c) (McKinney 1972). In Nebraska, the statute authorizes the adoption of regulations regarding educating the profession. **Neb.** Rev. Stat. §71-647 (3) (1981).

108. **Ala.** Code §22-10A-2 (b) (1) (1984); **Ark.** Stat. Ann. 82-626 (4), (7) (Supp. 1983); **Cal.** Health & Safety Code §309 (West Supp. 1984); **Colo.** Rev. Stat. §§25-4-1003 (2) (f), -(1) (d); §25-4-803 (2) (1982); **Hawaii** Rev. Stat. §333-11 (2) (1984) (discretionary for department to establish); **Idaho** Code §§39-910 (4), (6) (1977); **Ill.** Ann. Stat. ch. 111½, §4904 (a) (Smith-Hurd 1983); **Ind.** Code Ann. §16-8-6-2 (Burns 1983); **Iowa** Code Ann. §§136A.3 (2), (5), (6) (West Supp. 1984-5); **Kan.** Stat. Ann. §65-180 (a) (1980); **Mo.** Ann. Stat. §210.065.3 (Vernon 1983); **N.J.** Stat. Ann. §26:2-111 (West Supp. 1982-1983); §26:5B-4d (1983); **N.M.** Stat. Ann. §24-1-6 (c) (Supp. 1982); **N.D.** Cent Code §25-17-01 (1) (1978); **Okla.** Stat. Ann. tit. 63, §1-533 (West Supp. 1982-83); **Ore.** Rev. Stat. §433.290 (1981); **S.D.** Codified Laws Ann. §34-24-16 (Supp. 1984); and **Tenn.** Code Ann. §§68-5-301, -306 (1983).

109. **N.C.** Gen. Stat. §143B-196 (1983).

110. **N.C.** Gen. Stat. §143B-196 (1983); and **Ohio** Rev. Code Ann. §3701.502 (A) (Baldwin 1984).

111. **D.C.** Code Ann. §6-318 (1981); **Kan.** Stat. Ann. §65-180 (b) (1980); and **Va.** Code §32.1-72 (1982); §32.1-67 (Supp. 1984). Additionally, Georgia's statute provides that phenylketonuria and sickle cell anemia treatment is free, and that to the extent federal funds are available, the health department will provide for diagnosis and treatment. **Ga.** Code Ann. §§31-12-7 (b), 31-12-6 (d) (1982) In another area of cost, Michigan regulations provide that the Guthrie test shall be provided without charge by the department to all Michigan physicians and hospitals. **Mich.** Admin. Code R. §325.1471.

112. **N.C.** Gen Stat. §143B-194 and -195 (1973).

113. **Ark.** §82-626 (3) (Supp. 1983) (department may promulgate regualtion regarding cost); **Cal.** Health & Safety Code §309 (West Supp. 1984); **Cal.** Admin. Code tit. 17, R. 6504(f); **Colo.** Rev. Stat. §§25-4-1003 (1) (c), (2) (a), -1004 (2) (1983); **Idaho** regulations §2-12105.01 (d) (1980); **Ill.** Ann. Stat. ch. 111½, §§4904 (c), (d), (e) (Smith-Hurd 1983); **Ky.** Rev. Stat. §214-155 (1) (1982); **N.J.** Stat. Ann. §26:2-111 (West Supp. 1982-1983); **Ohio** Admin. Code §3701-49-01 (A) and (B) (1981); **Okla.** Stat. Ann. tit. 63, §1-534 (West Supp. 1982-1983); **Ore.** Rev. Stat. §§433.285 (2), (4) (1981). **Ore.** Admin. R. 333-24-240 (5) (a) (1983); **Utah** Code Ann. §26-10-6 (Supp. 1981); and **Wash.** Admin. Code R. 248-102-070, -040 (3) (1980).

Ohio[114] and California,[115] by regulation, specify the exact fee to be charged--$6 and $24, respectively.

The California regulation specifically provides that the fees collected shall be deposited in the Genetic Disease Testing Fund,[116] so that the money is not just deposited in the state treasury for use on projects other than genetics projects. Similarly, money collected in Colorado shall be credited to the newborn screening and genetic counseling and education programs[117] and money collected in Illinois shall be credited to the Metabolic Screening and Treatment Fund to be used solely for the purposes of providing metabolic screening, follow-up and treatment programs.[118]

The Oregon regulations require that the person responsible for submitting the sample pay a fee of $4.40 per specimen,[119] but the practitioner or patient may claim an exemption from this fee by asserting an inability to pay.[120] The Rhode Island guidelines and the Alaska regulations specify that the Department of Health will provide necessary materials and laboratory analyses for phenylketonuria testing at no charge.[121] A Texas statute addresses an additional means of financing newborn screening. It provides that the department may receive gifts and donations on behalf of the hypothyroidism screening program.[122]

Research

Only a minority of the newborn screening statutes address the issue of research. In California, the Genetic Disease Unit is authorized to make grants for demonstration projects to determine the desirability and feasibility of additional tests or new genetic services.[123] Similarly, a Birth Defects Institute is established by law in Iowa and New York to conduct investigations and research about the causes, mortality, methods or treatment, prevention and cure of birth defects and related diseases.[124]

114. **Ohio** Admin. Code §3701-49-01(A) (1983).

115. **Cal.** Admin. Code tit. 17 R. 6504(f) (1980).

116. **Cal.** Admin. Code tit. 17 R. 6504 (f) (1980).

117. **Colo.** Rev. Stat. §25-4-1006 (1983).

118. **Ill.** Ann. Stat. ch. 111½, §4904 (e) (Smith-Hurd 1983).

119. **Or.** Admin. R. 333-24-240(1)(a) (1983).

120. **Or.** Admin. R. 333-24-240(5)(a) (1983).

121. **Alaska** Admin. Code tit. 7 §27.540 (1983); and **R.I.** Dept. of Health, "Notice" 2 (1964) (on request).

122. **Tx.** Rev. Civ. Stat. Ann. art. 4447e-1 §10 (Vernon Supp. 1984).

123. **Cal.** Health & Safety Code §309 (West Supp. 1984).

124. **Iowa** Code Ann. §§136A.2, 136A.3 (1) (West Supp. 1984-1985); **N.Y.** Pub. Health Law §2732 (a) (McKinney 1972); and **N.Y.** Pub. Health Law §2731 (McKinney 1972).

To assure dissemination of the results of its work, the Institute is mandated to publish its results and surveys for the benefit of the public health, and collate such publications for distribution to scientific organizations and qualified scientists and physicians.[125] In Louisiana, the Department of Health and Human Resources' laboratory will conduct experiments, projects, and other undertakings as may be necessary to develop tests or ways to prevent or treat various enumerated diseases.[126] In Nebraska, a birth defects act (separate from the newborn screening law) empowers the Department of Health to conduct scientific investigations and surveys of the causes of mortality, methods of prevention, treatment and cure of birth defects.[127]

In Texas, the Department of Health is required to establish a laboratory for conducting experiments and projects necessary to develop the means to prevent and treat heritable diseases in children.[128] The regulations provide for data collection to derive incidence and prevalence rates.[129]

Continuing Monitoring of Program

Some states have attempted to assure an on-going monitoring of their programs, either through the establishment of advisory commissions[130] or through annual reports to the state legislature on the status of the program.[131] Other states have housed their newborn screening programs in a Birth Defects Institute[132] in an apparent attempt to assure coordination of various aspects of the program.

Protection of Carriers or Affected Individuals

Widespread screening of individuals for genetic disorders and recording of genetic information about them could lead to the possibility of discrimination against those individuals who are carriers of genetic disorders or who are affected by them. In Nebraska, the law provides that the Director of Health may require that test results be

125. **Iowa** Code Ann. §136A.3 (2) (West Supp. 1984-1985); and **N.Y.** Pub. Health Law §2732 (b) (McKinney 1972).

126. **La.** Rev. Stat. Ann. §40.1299 (West Supp. 1984).

127. **Neb.** Rev. Stat. Ann. §71-647 (1) (1981).

128. **Tx.** Rev. Civ. Stat. Ann. art. 4447e §1, 4447e-1 §1 (Vernon Supp. 1984).

129. **Texas** Department of Health, Maternal and Child Health Services, "Testing Newborn Children for Phenylketonuria, Other Heritable Diseases and Hypothyroidism" §37.59 (d) (1983).

130. **Md.** Pub. Health Code Ann. §13-103 et seq. (1982).

131. **Tenn.** Code Ann. §68-5-310 (1983).

132. **Iowa** Code Ann. §136A.2 (West Supp. 1984-1985).

recorded on the birth certificate.[133] Since birth certificates receive fairly wide dissemination (for example, to schools, passport offices, and so forth), there is a possibility of stigmatization if actual test results are recorded on them. Colorado takes what appears to be a more reasonable approach by providing that the birth certificate must indicate if phenylketonuria testing was done and state the type of test performed, but not the result.[134]

Some states have developed direct or indirect means of combatting genetic discrimination. The Washington, D.C., law provides that carriers of metabolic disorders should not be discriminated against by any person.[135] The Maryland law provides that the State Commission on Hereditary Disorders may investigate and make any necessary recommendation to end any unjustified discrimination that might result from identification of an individual as a carrier of a hereditary disorder.[136] The New Jersey statute focuses on affected individuals, rather than carriers. It provides that the Department of Health shall consult with the Commissioner of Insurance in identifying arbitrary and unreasonable discrimination against people with hereditary disorders and their families in insurance coverage.[137] Another New Jersey statute prohibits employers from discriminating based on an "atypical cellular blood type."[138]

Expansion of Genetics Services Programs

Now is an appropriate time to closely analyze the state genetics services because the programs are expanding. Not only are additional disorders being screened for, but additional types of services are being instituted or contemplated. In Alabama, for example, one of the objectives of the genetics law is to encourage prevention of birth defects through genetic counseling and amniocentesis.[139] To that end, the statute requires two university services to expand their programs to provide genetic counseling and prenatal testing.[140] Similarly, a California statute establishes a program of voluntary amniocentesis.[141] A related Oregon statute provides that it

133. **Neb.** Rev. Stat. §71-604.01(3) (1981).

134. 5 **Colo.** Code Reg: 1005-4 (II) (3) (1971).

135. **D.C.** Code Ann. §6-314 (1) (1981).

136. **Md.** Pub. Health Code Ann. §13-108 (4) (1982) The law specifically provides that this does not affect the individual's right to other forms of redress.

137. **N.J.** Stat. Ann. §26:5B-4 (e) (West Supp. 1982-1983).

138. **N.J.** Stat. Ann. §10:5-12 (West Supp. 1982-1983).

139. **Ala.** Code §22-10A-1 (1984); see also **N.J.** Stat. Ann. §10:5-12 (West Supp. 1982-1983).

140. **Ala.** Code §22-10A-2 (a) (1984) (at the University of Alabama and the University of South Alabama, specifically).

141. **Cal.** Health & Safety Code §290 (1979).

is state policy to encourage amniocentesis[142] and provides that the university establish a graduated fee schedule, develop an educational program for physicians and the public, assure that genetic counseling is given in conjunction with the amniocentesis, and provide that participation shall be voluntary.[143]

Only a few states, at the regulatory level, are addressing the issue of maternal phenylketonuria. A California regulation provides that after an initial presumptive positive phenylketonuria result on a newborn, a blood specimen shall also be obtained on the newborn's mother.[144] A North Dakota policy statement provides that the Division of Maternal and Child Health will provide information and counseling regarding the issue of maternal phenylketonuria for young women with phenylketonuria who are anticipating childbearing.[145] The statement does not provide a means for identifying which women have maternal phenylketonuria, however. The Louisiana guidelines provide for phenylketonuria testing of pregnant women who are mentally retarded or have a family history of phenylketonuria[146] and for such testing of family members of a known case of phenylketonuria or familial mental retardation.[147] None of the laws or regulations provide for the contacting of women of child bearing age who as infants had been diagnosed as having phenylketonuria.

As states expand their programs to include not only newborn screening, but also services for pregnant women, such as amniocentesis or phenylketonuria screening, important ethical issues arise regarding the extent to which the services will affect the decision whether or not to continue the pregnancy. The legislatures in some states have been sensitive to the fundamentally personal nature of the decision to bear children and have articulated a state policy of not interfering with that decision. In Colorado, for example, the statute provides that "The extremely personal decision to bear children shall remain the free choice and responsibility of the individual and such free choice and responsibility shall not be restricted by any of the genetic services of the state. . . ."[148]

142. Or. Rev. Stat. §352.058 (1) (1981).

143. Or. Rev. Stat. §352.058 (4) (1981).

144. Cal. Admin. Code tit. 17 R. 6504 (d) (1980).

145. N.D. Dept. of Health Division of Maternal and Child Health, "Newborn Metabolic Screening Policy Statement" (November 1982).

146. La. Dept. of Health and Human Resources, "Guidelines: Neonatal Screening Programs" §III (D) (1).

147. La. Dept. of Health and Human Resources: "Guidelines: Neonatal Screening Programs." §III (D) (3).

148. Col. Rev. Stat. §25-4-1003 (2) (d) (1983).

State Newborn Screening Laws

ALABAMA

I. **Is there a statute addressing neonatal genetic screening?** Ala. Code § 22-10A-1 et seq. (1984) and § 22-20-3 (1984).

A. **Does it state an objective?** "[T]o identify families who have members with genetic disorders that cause birth defects and mental retardation" and "to encourage prevention of birth defects and mental retardation through education, genetic counseling and amniocentesis when applicable." § 22-§ 10A-1

B. **Does it compel screening?** Mandatory newborn screening § 22-20-3(a), but genetic counseling and amniocentesis shall be voluntary and shall not be a prerequisite to eligibility for or receipt of any other service or assistance from any other program. § 22-10A-3

1. **Are there exceptions?** Parents may object on religious grounds. § 22-20-3(a)

2. **Does it provide notice to parents and guardians of the right to object?** No mention.

II. **What does the program screen for and how readily can other tests be added?** Hypothyroidism and phenylketonuria. § 22-20-3(a)

III. **Does the statute provide for centralization or quality assurance?** The University of Alabama in Birmingham, through its laboratory of medical genetics, and the University of South Alabama, shall expand their respective medical genetics program to provide diagnostic facilities, genetic counseling and prenatal testing for genetic disorders. § 22-10A-2(a)

IV. **Who is responsible . . .**

A. **For each individual screen?** The administrative officer or other persons in charge of each institution caring for infants 28 days or less of age, or the physician attending a newborn child, or the person attending a newborn child that was not attended by a physician. § 22-20-3(a)

B. **For the program?** The state Board of Health, which shall promulgate rules and regulations necessary to implement the legislation. § 22-20-3(b)

1. **Does the program provide for . . .**

a. **testing** Time and manner to be determined by board. § 22-20-3(a)

b. **confirming positive result** No mention.

c. **reporting** No mention.

d. **recording** The recording of the test results shall be performed at such times and in such manner as prescribed by the board. § 22-20-3(a)

e. **treatment** The board shall promulgate such rules and regulations as it considers necessary for the care and treatment of those newborns whose tests are positive, including advising dietary treatment. § 22-20-3(b)

f. **follow-up** No mention.

g. **education** The medical genetics program is charged with developing an education program for physicians and the public concerning genetic disorders and the availability of the program. § 22-10A-2(b)(1) Also, the program shall assist private physicians and clinics of the Dept. of Public Health in referring affected members and their families to the program. § 22-10A-2(c)

h. **counseling** The medical genetics program will assure that genetic counseling is available to those Alabama families who need it. § 22-10A-2(b)(2)

i. **research** No mention.

j. **other** The state Board of Health shall promulgate any other rules and regulations necessary to effectuate the provisions of this section. § 22-20-3(b)

2. **Are there confidentiality requirements?** No mention.

3. **Is a registry established?** No mention.

C. **For the costs of the program?** For the services provided by the universities, the medical genetics program shall formulate a graduated fee schedule, based on the patient's ability to pay to offset the costs of the program. § 22-10A-2(b)(3) No specific mention of how newborn screening is funded.

V. **Are there sanctions to punish non-compliance?** No mention.

ALASKA

I. **Is there a statute addressing neonatal genetic screening?** Alaska Stat. § 18.15.200 (1981). Regulations are set forth in Alaska Admin. Code tit. 7 § 27.510 et seq.

A. **Does it state an objective?** No mention.

B. **Does it compel screening?** Mandatory § 18.15.200(a)

1. **Are there exceptions?** Parental or guardian refusal. The refusal shall be reported to the department. § 18.15.200(f) See also regulations § 27.530(e).

2. **Does it provide notice to parents and guardians of the right to object?** No mention.

II. **What does the program screen for and how readily can other tests be added?** Phenylketonuria and other heritable diseases as tests become available. § 18.15.200(a), (f). See also regulations § 27.510.

III. **Does the statute provide for centralization or quality assurance?** Follow up tests shall be made at a laboratory approved by the department. § 18.15.200(e) The regulations state that the department will provide physicians and nurses with specimen collection materials, reporting forms, and mailing containers which may be requested from the regional public health laboratory serving the area. § 27.540

IV. **Who is responsible . . .**

A. **For each individual screen?** A physician who attends a newborn, or if the mother delivers in the absence of a physician, the nurse who first visits the child. § 18.15.200(a) The regulations add that the responsibility of specimen collecting may be delegated to appropriate nursery, laboratory, or office staff. § 27.520

B. **For the program?** The Department of Health and Social Services. § 18.15.200(b)

1. **Does the program provide for . . .**

a. **testing** The department shall prescibe regulations regarding the method used and the time or times of testing. § 18.15.200(b) The necessary laboratory tests shall be provided by the department. § 18.15.200(c) The regulations specify that one specimen should be collected between 48 hours and 7 days of age (§ 27.530(1)) or if this is not possible, two specimens should be collected, the first before 48 hours of age and the second before 21 days of age. § 27.530(2)

b. **confirming positive result** When presumptive positive screening tests have been reported to the department it shall provide, on request, either the true blood phenylalanine test or subsidize its performance at an approved laboratory. § 18.15.200(e) The regulations state that the department will provide for confirmatory laboratory testing upon the request of the physician. § 27.560

c. **reporting** A confirmed diagnosis of phenylketonuria shall be reported to the physician and to the department. § 18.15.200(d) The regulations require that any positive or abnormal results requiring immediate action be reported by telephone to the infant's physician. § 27.550(c)

d. **recording** No mention.

e. **treatment** The department shall provide services for treatment of any diagnosed case. § 18.15.200(d) The regulations state that formal application for clinical diagnostic and for treatment services must be made to the Handicapped Children's Program of the Division of Public Health. § 27.560

f. **follow-up** The department shall provide services for clinical follow-up of any diagnosed case. § 18.15.200(d)

g. **education** No mention.

h. **counseling** No mention.

i. **research** No mention.

j. **other** The necessary laboratory tests and the test materials, reporting forms and mailing cartons shall be provided by the department. § 18.15.200(c)

2. **Are there confidentiality requirements?** No mention.

3. **Is a registry established?** Another statute provides the department will keep a case registry of persons who have impairments. § 18.05.044(a) (1974)

a. **Is it mandatory?** No person with an impairment or the parent or guardian of such a person may be compelled to furnish or consent to furnishing information requested for the case registry. No private or governmental organization, institution, or individual may furnish information to the registry without the written consent of the person or his parent or guardian. § 18.05.044(b)

b. **Is it confidential?** There shall be no disclosure which would identify a registered person with an impairment except to those agencies or individuals authorized by the commissioner and who are engaged in the provision of services or research to improve the condition of the impaired. § 18.05.046(a) Any such information and any findings based upon such information shall remain confidential. § 18.05.046(b)

C. **For the costs of the program?** No mention in the statute. The regulations state that testing materials and reporting forms shall be supplied to physicians without cost. § 27.540

V. **Are there sanctions to punish non-compliance?** Fine of not more than $500; however, a person whose request for specimens is denied by the parents or guardian is not guilty of a misdemeanor. § 18.15.200(f)

ARIZONA

I. **Is there a statute addressing neonatal genetic screening?** Ariz. Rev. Stat. Ann. § 36-694B (Supp. 1983). Regulations are set forth in Ariz. Admin. Comp. R9-14-511 et seq. (1979).

A. **Does it state an objective?** Regulations describe the purpose as causing newborns "to be tested for metabolic disorders for which early and appropriate treatment can provide prevention or substantial amelioration of mental retardation." R9-14-511 (B)

B. **Does it compel screening?** Mandatory § 36-694B.

1. **Are there exceptions?** Parental refusal R9-14-511 (B). Such refusal must be documented in the newborn's medical records. R9-14-515

2. **Does it provide notice to parents and guardians of the right to object?** No mention.

II. **What does the program screen for and how readily can other tests be added?** Tests for metabolic disorders § 36-694B. Those specified in the regulations are phenylketonuria, galactosemia, and hypothyroidism. R9-14-513

III. **Does the statute provide for centralization or quality assurance?** No mention.

IV. **Who is responsible . . .**

A. **For each individual screen?** The attending physician or other person required to make a report on the birth. § 36-694B. The regulations additionally make the person in charge of the institution or his designated representative responsible for assuring that the newborn medical record indicates that the tests were ordered or the parents refused. R9-14-514(2)

B. **For the program?** The Department of Health Services shall specify rules and regulations consistent with the recommendations of a metabolic screening committee. § 36-694B

1. **Does the program provide for . . .**

a. **testing** Tests specified by department rules and regulations shall be reviewed at least annually by the committee. § 36-694B The regulations provide for screening to be done when the infant is three days of age or at time of discharge (whichever is earlier) and for specimens to be sent to a designated laboratory within 24 hours. R9-14-513 A, B

b. confirming positive result No mention.

c. reporting No mention.

d. recording No mention.

e. treatment No mention.

f. follow-up No mention.

g. education No mention.

h. counseling No mention.

i. research No mention.

2. Are there confidentiality requirements? No mention.

3. Is a registry established? No mention.

C. For the costs of the program? No mention.

V. Are there sanctions to punish non-compliance? No mention.

ARKANSAS

I. **Is there a statute addressing neonatal genetic screening?** Ark. Stat. Ann. §§ 82-625, 82-626 (Supp. 1983). The State Board of Health has adopted Rules and Regulations Pertaining to the Testing of Newborn Infants for Phenylketonuria and Hypothyroidism (July 13, 1984).

A. **Does it state an objective?** No mention in the statute. The rules state as their purpose to provide a method to assure that all newborn infants are tested for phenylketonuria and hypothyroidism and to assure that all newborns detected as abnormal receive appropriate medical follow up. § 1

B. **Does it compel screening?** Mandatory. § 86-625

1. **Are there exceptions?** No mention.

2. **Does it provide notice to parents and guardians of the right to object?** No mention.

II. **What does the program screen for and how readily can other tests be added?** Phenylketonuria and hypothyroidism. § 86-625

III. **Does the statute provide for centralization or quality assurance?** The State Dept. of Health shall establish, equip, and staff a central laboratory. § 82-626(5) The regulations provide that the Department of Health shall be responsible for providing forms and instructions for blood tests, processing and recording the samples received, and analysing samples within a reasonable period of time. § 3(B)

IV. **Who is responsible . . .**

A. **For each individual screen?** The department will promulgate regulations in conjunction with the Insurance Commissioner establishing what persons and institutions shall be required to obtain specimens. § 82-626(3)(a) According to the regulations it is the responsibility of the physician attending birth and, if the birth occurs in a medical facility, the medical facility in which birth occurs to assure that the proper procedures for testing are followed. § 3(A)(1)(2) Where birth occurs without an attending physician, it is the responsibility of the person in attendence to see that a blood sample is taken and submitted. § 3(A)(3) For infants under six months of age who come to the attention of the department as not having been tested, it is the responsibility of the Department to collect blood samples. § 3(A)(4)

B. For the program? The State Department of Health. § 82-626

1. Does the program provide for . . .

a. testing The department will prescribe the test or tests that may be administered and the procedures and manner of testing. § 82-625, § 82-626(2) The regulations provide extensive guidelines for the collection and submission of blood samples. § 4 For healthy births a blood specimen shall be collected at the time of discharge or within seven days, whichever is sooner. A repeat test is required if sample is collected within 24 hours of birth. § 4(A)(1)

b. confirming positive result No mention in the statute. The regulations require prompt follow-up testing for presumptive positive results on phenylketonuria tests. § 6(A)(2)

c. reporting The central laboratory will report findings resulting from the tests. § 82-626(5) All positive test results shall be sent immediately to the department. § 82-625, § 82-626(6) The regulations require that abnormal results shall be reported to the submitter as soon as possible after detection. §§ 5(A), 6(A)(2)

d. recording No mention in the statute. According to the regulations, the Department is responsible for the processing and recording of samples received. § 3(B)

e. treatment The department shall assist in treatment and care of affected infants. § 82-626(6) The regulations require that dietary therapy be instituted after diagnosis of phenylketonuria (§ 7(C)) and that replacement therapy with thyroid hormone be instituted for children affected by congenital hypothyroidism (§ 7(D)).

f. follow-up Follow-up procedures to begin no later than (10) ten days from the positive diagnosis. § 82-626(6)

g. education The department shall furnish copies of the statute and regulations to physicians, hospitals and others responsible for screening. § 82-626(4). The department will disseminate information and advice to the public concerning the dangers and effects of phenylketonuria and hypothyroidism. § 82-626(7)

h. counseling No mention.

i. research No mention.

2. Are there confidentiality requirements? No mention.

3. **Is a registry established?** No mention in the statute. The regulations require that the Department maintain a registry to record the results of diagnosis and to track referral for those infants with abnormal test results. § 7(B)

   a. **Is it mandatory?** Yes.

   b. **Is it confidential?** No mention.

C. **For the costs of the program?** The department, in conjunction with the Insurance Commissioner, shall establish the amount to be charged by the central laboratory and the method of billing such charges to the persons and institutions. § 82-626(3)

V. **Are there sanctions to punish non-compliance?** The department will enforce the provisions of this act. § 82-626(1)

CALIFORNIA

I. **Is there a statute addressing neonatal genetic screening?** Cal. Health and Safety Code § 309 (West Supp. 1984). The regulations are set forth in Cal. Admin. Code tit. 17, R.6500.5 et seq. (1980).

A. **Does it state an objective?** To make every effort to detect, as early as possible, phenylketonuria and other preventable heritable disorders leading to mental retardation or physical defects. § 309

B. **Does it compel screening?** Mandatory. § 309; R.6501(a) (regulations)

1. **Are there exceptions?** A parent or guardian may object on religious grounds. § 309; R.6501(b) (regulations) According to the regulations, refusal shall be made in writing and included in the newborn's medical or hospital record. R.6501(c)(2); R.6505(m)

2. **Does it provide notice to parents and guardians of the right to object?** No mention in the statute. According to the regulations, all birth attendants engaged in providing perinatal care shall provide pregnant women, prior to the estimated date of delivery, with a copy of informational material, titled "Important Information for Parents," provided by the department concerning state-mandated newborn screening tests. R.6505(h) If this does not occur, the health facility admitting the pregnant woman for delivery shall provide the material. If the woman is unable to read it, the material shall be translated or read to her in a language she understands. R.6505(c)

II. **What does the program screen for and how readily can other tests be added?** Phenylketonuria and other preventable heritable disorders. The statute authorizes study to see if tests for galactosemia, histidinemia, galactokinase deficiency, homocystinuria, maple syrup urine disease, hypothyroidism, and tyrosinosis should be implemented. § 309 The regulations provide for screening for phenylketonuria, hypothyroidism and galactosemia. R.6501(a)

III. **Does the statute provide for centralization or quality assurance?** The state shall perform laboratory services including quality control. § 309 The state department may provide laboratory testing facilities or contract with any laboratory which it deems qualified to conduct tests. § 309 The criteria for approval are set forth in the regulations. R.6503 The regulations also require the hospital to review each newborn's medical record within 14 days from discharge to determine that the tests were done and the results recorded. R.6505(d) If the testing was not done, the hospital must immediately call the newborn's physician and send written notification to the physician and the department. If the physician is unavailable, a state-approved genetic consultant must be notified. R.6505(e)

IV. Who is responsible . . .

A. For each individual screen? No mention in the statute. According to the regulations, physicians or birth attendants in health facilities shall have the specimens collected. R.6505(i) If the infant is not born in a health facility or admitted to one before six days of age, the birth attendant or physician shall have a blood specimen collected. R.6505(j)

B. For the program? The state Department of Health shall establish a genetic disease unit which shall coordinate all programs of the state department in the area of genetic disease and which shall designate tests and regulations. § 309

1. Does the program provide for . . .

a. testing The designated tests shall be in accordance with accepted medical practices. § 309 The regulations provide guidelines for the timing of tests (R.6501(c), R.6505(i), (k)) and require the department to develop and make available criteria for the collection of specimens, the interpretation of tests, and abnormal test results. R.6502(c) It is the department's responsibility to establish blood concentrations or test results defined as positive for reporting. R.6504(c) Specimens in appropriate containers shall be placed in the United States mail or other approved channel of transmittal to the assigned, state-approved laboratory as soon as possible, but not later than 12 hours after they have been obtained. R.6505(q) According to the regulations, a newborn's physician who is notified by the laboratory by telephone that a specimen is inadequate shall make every reasonable effort to have an adequate specimen obtained within five days of notification. If he or she cannot obtain the specimen, he or she shall notify the area genetic center as soon as possible by telephone. Such telephone notification shall be noted in the newborn's physician's records specifying the date of notification, the person notified, and the information provided. R.6505(n) A similar procedure shall take place when the newborn's physician is notified by telephone that a newborn was discharged from the health facility before a specimen was taken. R.6505(o)

Each local health department in the country where the newborn resides shall be responsible for making every reasonable effort to obtain specimens when requested by the state-approved area genetic center consultant or the department. If, after every reasonable effort, a specimen cannot be obtained, the local health department may terminate efforts after 30 days (with approval from the department). R.6506

b. **confirming positive result** The state department shall perform confirmatory laboratory services. § 309 According to the regulations, initial presumptive positive test results for phenylketonuria and galactosemia shall in all cases be followed by a recall blood specimen. For all initial presumptive positive phenylketonuria tests, a blood specimen shall also be obtained on the newborn's mother. R.6504(d) When the newborn's physician is notified by telephone by the State-approved area genetic consultant of an initial presumptive positive test result for galactosemia or phenylketonuria, the newborn's physician shall obtain an adequate blood specimen from the newborn and in the case of presumptive positive phenylketonuria test result, from the newborn's mother, and submit these specimens to a State-approved laboratory within 48 hours. If the blood specimen cannot be obtained and submitted within 48 hours, the newborn's physician shall notify the area genetic center by telephone. Such telephone notification shall be noted in the newborn's physician's records, specifying the date of notification, the person notified and the information provided. R.6505(p)

c. **reporting** No mention in the statutes. According to the regulations, all physicians making an initial diagnosis of a preventable heritable disorder for which testing is required shall report such diagnosis and information necessary for follow-up and investigation to the department. R.6505(r)

d. **recording** No mention in the statute. According to the regulations, the department shall develop and require perinatal licensed health facilities to purchase and use appropriate specimen collection forms for the collection of the blood specimen and the recording of test results. R.6504(a) The specimen record forms shall be fully and accurately completed by birth attendants, perinatal licensed health facilities and laboratories and shall be filed in each newborn's medical record. R.6504(b)

e. **treatment** Another statute, the "Genetically Handicapped Person's Program," § 340-348, has exhaustive measures for treatment, including funding for surgery and habilitation.

f. **follow-up** No mention.

g. **education** The state genetic disease unit shall promote a statewide program of testing information. The department shall inform all hospitals or physicians or both of the required regulations or tests. § 309

h. **counseling** The state genetic disease unit shall promote a statewide program of counseling services. § 309

i. **research** The genetic disease unit is authorized to make grants for demonstration projects to determine the desirability and feasibility of additional tests or new genetic services. § 309

j. **other** The state department shall perform laboratory services including quality control and emergency testing. § 309 Another statute, Cal. Health and Safety Code § 290 (1979), establishes a program of voluntary amniocentesis for genetic disorders.

2. **Are there confidentiality requirements?** No mention in the statute. According to the regulations, health facility records on newborn screening are confidential, but open to the department for program administration purposes. R.6505(g)

3. **Is a registry established?** No mention.

C. **For the costs of the program?** Provision of laboratory testing facilities shall be contingent on the provision of funding. The state department shall charge a fee for any tests performed, the amount to be established, and periodically adjusted by the State Director of Health Services. § 309 According to the regulations, the department shall determine a fee for each specimen record form provided. The fee shall be twenty-four dollars ($24). All fees collected shall be deposited in the Genetic Disease Testing Fund. R.6504(f) The cost of the specimen record forms shall be determined by the department. R.6505(a) The health facility shall make available at no additional charge specimen collection services or a specimen record form to the physician responsible for obtaining either a repeat specimen for an inadequate specimen or a specimen on a newborn discharged without the test being obtained. R.6504(f) The Department shall supply forms for the collection of the blood specimen at no cost for recall tests, and for tests on mothers of newborns with an initial presumptive positive phenylketonuria test. R.6504(e)

V. **Are there sanctions to punish non-compliance?** No mention in the statute. According to the regulations, willful or repeated failure to comply with these regulations shall be referred by the Department to the appropriate licensing authority. Such failure may constitute grounds for disciplinary action including revocation of license. R.6505(s).

COLORADO

I. **Is there a statute addressing neonatal genetic screening?** Colo. Rev. Stat. § 25-4-801 et seq. (1982) and § 25-4-1001 et seq. (1983). Regulations are set forth at 5 Colo. Code Reg. 1005-4 (1977).

A. **Does it state an objective?** To prevent mental retardation resulting from phenylketonuria and other metabolic defects and inform people of the nature and effects of such defects. § 25-4-801 To assure state policy regarding newborn screening and genetic counseling is made with full public knowledge, in light of expert opinion and be constantly reviewed. § 25-4-1002(1)(a) To assure participation in genetic counseling is voluntary and information is confidential. § 25-4-1002(1)(b)

B. **Does it compel screening?** Mandatory. 25-4-802

1. **Are there exceptions?** A parent who is a member of a well-recognized church or whose religious tenets oppose treatment may object on religious grounds. § 25-4-804, § 25-4-1005.
Parents may object for personal reasons. § 25-4-1005
Genetic counseling is voluntary. § 25-4-1003(2)(b)

2. **Does it provide notice to parents and guardians of the right to object?** No mention.

II. **What does the program screen for and how readily can other tests be added?** Phenylketonuria, hypothyroidism, abnormal hemoglobins, galactosemia, homocystinuria, maple syrup urine disease. § 25-4-1004(1)

III. **Does the statute provide for centralization or quality assurance?** Laboratories are operated by or approved by the Department of Health. § 25-4-802(1) Newborn screening shall be provided in the most efficient and cost-effective manner possible. § 25-4-1003(2)(a) Newborn screening and diagnostic services should be carried out under adequate standards of supervision and quality control. § 25-4-1003(2)(a) Under the regulations, the laboratory must be directed full time by a clinical pathologist (5 CCR 1005-4 (III)(1)(a)), and testing must be done under the immediate supervision of the clinical pathologist lab director. 5 CCR 1005-4 (III)(1)(c) Also, the department can withdraw approval of a laboratory after giving the director notice of deficiencies and providing one month for the necessary corrections to be made. 5 CCR 1005-4 (III)(1)(e)

IV. Who is responsible . . .

A. For each individual screen? Either the chief medical staff officer or other person in charge of each institution caring for newborn infants, or, if a newborn infant is not born in an institution or is discharged prior to the time prescribed for taking the specimen, the person responsible for signing the birth certificate of such child shall obtain a specimen. § 25-4-802(1)

The physician, nurse midwife, or other health professional attending a birth outside a hospital. § 25-4-1004(1) Under the regulations, a local health officer or representative of the health department may cause a sample to be taken if none has been obtained. 5 CCR 1005-4 (II)(2)(a). The birth certificate must indicate if phenylketonuria testing was done and state the type of test. 5 CCR 1005-4 (II)(3)

B. For the program? The State Board of Health and the Department of Health shall prescribe the tests, manner of performance and reporting of results. § 25-4-802(2)(3)

The executive director of the Department of Health shall establish and administer the program for newborn screening, genetic counseling and education, including promulgating rules and regulations. § 25-4-1003(1)

1. Does the program provide for . . .

a. testing The state board shall periodically prescribe which tests shall be done in such manner and at such times and places as prescribed by the Department of Health. § 25-4-802(2)(3) Under the regulations, tests must be performed by the laboratory within a week of receipt. 5 CCR 1005-4 (III)(3) The board shall promulgate rules and regulations concerning obtaining samples and their handling and delivery for testing. § 25-4-803(1)

The regulations specify what are negative tests, positive tests and unsatisfactory specimens. 5 CCR 1005-4(I)(4)-(6) Tests must be performed no sooner than 24 hours after onset of milk feeding and as late as possible before discharge. 5 CCR 1005-4 (II)(1)(a) Premature infants must be tested at one week of age and upon discharge. 5 CCR 1005-4 (III)(3)(a) Siblings in known phenylketonuria families must be tested at one week, two weeks and six weeks. 5 CCR 1005-4 (III)(3)(b)

b. confirming positive result It is the duty of the department to contact as soon as possible all cases suspected of having any such disorders or defects and to do any additional testing required to confirm or disprove the suspected disorder. § 25-4-802(4)

c. **reporting** The reporting of results shall be done as prescribed by the department. § 25-4-802(3) Under the regulations, negative results are reported weekly to the hospital and physician. 5 CCR 1005-4 (III)(4) Positive results are reported to the hospital, physician, and Director of Child Health Services. 5 CCR 1005-4 (III)(4)

   The results of the testing shall be forwarded to the physician for communication to the parent. § 25-4-1004(1)

d. **recording** The executive director shall establish systems for recording information obtained in newborn screening. § 25-4-1003(1)(e)

e. **treatment** No mention.

f. **follow-up** No mention.

g. **education** Information on the operation of all programs shall be open and freely available to the public. § 25-4-1003(2)(f) The department "shall furnish all physicians, public health nurses, hospitals, maternity homes, and departments of social services available medical information concerning the nature and effects of phenylketonuria and other metabolic defects found likely to cause mental retardation." § 25-4-803(2)

   The executive director of the Department of Health shall gather and disseminate information to further the public's understanding of newborn screening and education and counseling programs. § 25-4-1003(1)(d).

h. **counseling** The executive director of the department shall establish programs and promulgate rules for a genetic counseling program § 25-4-1003(1)(a)(b) and gather and disseminate information to further the public's understanding of the counseling program. § 25-4-1003(1)(d) Participation is voluntary. § 25-4-1002(b) Genetic counseling services shall be available to persons in need, shall be non-directive and shall emphasize informing the client. § 25-4-1003(2)(c)

   "All participants in programs on genetic counseling and education shall be informed of the nature of possible risks involved in participation in such a program or project, and shall be informed of the nature and cost of available therapies or maintenance programs for those affected by hereditary disorders, and shall be informed of the possible benefits and risks of such therapies and programs. . . ." § 25-4-1003(2)(g)

No hospital or other health facility or any physician or other health professional is required to provide genetic counseling "beyond the usual and customary and accepted practice nor shall any hospital or other health facility be held liable for not providing such genetic counseling." § 25-4-1003(2)(h)

i. **research** No mention.

j. **other** The statute provides that "The extremely personal decision to bear children shall remain the free choice and responsibility of the individual and such free choice and responsibility shall not be restricted by any of the genetic services of the state. . . ." § 25-4-1003(2)(d)

2. **Are there confidentiality requirements?** All information gathered by the department of health or by other agencies, entities and individuals conducting programs on newborn screening and genetic counseling and education, other than statistical information and information which the individual allows to be released through his informed consent, shall be confidential. § 25-4-1003(2)(e) Information on the operation of the programs shall be open and freely available to the public. § 25-4-1003(2)(f)

   a. **Who has access?** Public and private access to individual patient data is limited to data compiled without the individual's name. § 25-4-1003(e)

3. **Is a registry established?** No mention.

C. **For the costs of the program?** The executive director shall fix reasonable fees to be charged for services. § 25-4-1003(1)(c) Newborn screening shall be provided in the most efficient and cost-effective manner possible. § 25-4-1003(2)(a). The executive director shall assess a laboratory fee that is sufficient to cover the costs of such testing and hospitals shall assess a reasonable fee charged to the parents to cover the costs of handling of specimens. § 25-4-1004(2) All monies received from fees shall be credited to the newborn screening and genetic counseling and education programs by the state treasurer. § 25-4-1006

V. **Are there sanctions to punish non-compliance?** No mention.

CONNECTICUT

I. **Is there a statute addressing neonatal genetic screening?** Conn. Gen. Stat. Ann. § 19a-55 (West Supp. 1984). The State of Connecticut Department of Health Services provides regulations for screening set forth in Conn. Agencies Regs. §§ 19-13-D41, -D42 (1979).

A. **Does it state an objective?** No mention.

B. **Does it compel screening?** Mandatory. 19a-55(a)

1. **Are there exceptions?** Parents may object on religious grounds. 19a-55(b) The regulations make parental objection grounds for exception but do not clearly specify that the parents' objection must be on religious grounds. § 19-13-D41 A separate section requires that objections on religious grounds be made in writing and kept as part of the infant's hospital record. § 19-13-D42

2. **Does it provide notice to parents and guardians of the right to object?** No mention.

II. **What does the program screen for and how readily can other tests be added?** Phenylketonuria, hypothyroidism, galactosemia and other inborn errors of metabolism. 19a-55(a)

III. **Does the statute provide for centralization or quality assurance?** No mention. According to a statement from the Department of Health Services, hypothyroid testing is performed on a New England Regional basis at the Massachusett's Health Department laboratory and the tests for phenylketonuria and galactosemia are performed exclusively at the State of Connecticut Department of Health Services laboratory. The Health Code regulations state that specimen collection materials must be furnished by or acceptable to the department. § 19-13-D41(a)

IV. **Who is responsible . . .**

A. **For each individual screen?** The administrative officer or other person in charge of each institution caring for infants 28 days or less of age. § 19a-55(a); § 19-13-D41 (regulation)

B. **For the program?** The commissioner of health services, who shall adopt rules and regulations. § 19a-55(a)

1. **Does the program provide for . . .**

a. **testing** The commissioner shall adopt regulations specifying the abnormal conditions to be tested for and the manner in which they are to be performed. 19a-55(a) According to the regulations, specimens should not be collected until at least 24 hours after the first milk feeding unless the infant is discharged sooner in which case specimens should be taken not earlier than three hours before discharge. § 19-13-D41(b) Specimens shall be sent to a laboratory approved by the state within forty-eight hours after collection. § 19-13-D41(c)

b. **confirming positive result** No mention in the statute. According to the Department of Health Services statements, a second filter paper kit for a follow-up specimen is usually mailed out the day an abnormal result is received.

c. **reporting** To be specified by the commissioner. 19a-55(a) The regulations state that results of tests be transmitted to the department within twenty-four hours after the test. § 19-13-D41(f) According to the department statement, abnormal reports must be communicated to the Maternal and Child Health Section and one of their physicians contacts the pediatrician or clinic of the child by phone.

d. **recording** To be specified by the commissioner. 19a-55(a) The regulations require that the records must indicate the tests were performed and the results must be maintained for five years. § 19-13-D41(g)

e. **treatment** No mention.

f. **follow-up** No mention.

g. **education** No mention.

h. **counseling** No mention.

i. **research** No mention.

2. **Are there confidentiality requirements?** No mention.

3. **Is a registry established?** No mention. Under another law, health care professionals are required to report to the health department any child under age five who has a physical defect. § 19a-53

C. **For the costs of the program?** No mention.

V. **Are there sanctions to punish non-compliance?** No mention.

DELAWARE

I. **Is there a statute addressing newborn genetic screening?** No. Though there is no statute which addresses neonatal genetic screening, the Department of Health and Social Services' Division of Public Health has established a screening program for testing on a voluntary basis. It provides program and procedural guidelines for hospitals and health units as well as specimen collection materials and report forms. The following analysis of Delaware's screening program is made with reference to materials distributed by the Division of Public Health entitled "Hereditary Metabolic Disorders (HMD) Program-Guidelines" (January 1983).

A. **Does it state an objective?** To identify and treat various metabolic disorders.

B. **Does it compel screening?** No. This is a voluntary program. Health care professionals are informed of its voluntary nature in the guidelines and a pamphlet directed to parents makes it clear that there is no law requiring this test. However, there is no indication in the description of the program that the persons responsible for testing have an obligation to inform the parents that the program is voluntary.

II. **What does the program screen for and how readily can other tests be added?** Hypothyroidism, phenylketonuria, galactosemia, maple syrup urine disease and homocystinuria.

III. **Does the statute provide for centralization or quality assurance?** The Delaware Division of Public Health has a contract with the Laboratory of the Maryland Department of Mental Health and Hygiene to analyze blood specimens.

IV. **Who is responsible . . .**

A. **For each individual screen?** Though not stated explicitly, the guideines imply that the attending physician has responsibility for having the infant tested. If a repeat test is needed due to an unsatisfactory specimen or insufficient milk feeding, the public health nurses do the repeat test.

B. **For the program?** Department of Health and Social Services, Division of Public Health, Office of Maternal and Child Health Services.

1. **Does the program provide for . . .**

a. **testing** The guidelines recommend obtaining one blood specimen before discharge. If the specimen is taken before the infant has had 24 hours of milk feeding he or she is referred to a health unit for a second test. A "procedure manual" specifies testing guidelines for newborns on antibiotics, sick newborns with prolonged hospital stay, premature or low birth weight infants and for other infants where circumstances require a second test.

b. **confirming positive result** Arrangements are made for follow-up testing. Physicians may do certain tests at local laboratories.

c. **reporting** The Maryland laboratory sends all results to the Maternal and Child Health Services Office. Within 7 days of receipt, physicians are notified of all abnormal or suspicious test results. If an abnormal result warrants emergency follow-up, the laboratory notifies the physician immediately by phone.

d. **recording** The Maryland laboratory maintains a copy of the results of testing for each infant. Results are recorded and filed by the Maternal and Child Health Office.

e. **treatment** If the infant does not have a private physician, the department office notifies parents of abnormal test results and makes an appointment with a physician. Families can be referred to the Genetics Clinic of the Wilmington Medical Center which offers further testing and/or counseling on a sliding fee schedule according to patient's income.

f. **follow-up** If a suspected condition is confirmed, the office contacts the physician for periodic reports on the progress of the infant for at least one year. The department office will refer physicians to a metabolic specialist if requested.

g. **education** The education of the community is one of the objectives of the Genetics Unit.

h. **counseling** The Genetics Clinic of the Wilmington Medical Center offers counseling.

i. **research** No mention.

j. **other** The division provides for the Amish community's preference for home births by sending public health nurses to collect a sample in the home upon notification of a birth.

2. **Are there confidentiality requirements?** No mention.

3. **Is a registry established?** No mention except for the file which is maintained on each patient of the Division of Public Health.

C. **For the costs of the program?** The department does not provide any medical or financial coverage beyond detection. It does refer families to facilities which offer a sliding fee schedule for treatments.

V. **Are there sanctions to punish non-compliance?** The program is strictly voluntary.

DISTRICT OF COLUMBIA

I. **Is there a statute addressing neonatal genetic screening?** D.C. Code Ann. § 6-311 et seq. (1981).

A. **Does it state an objective?** To provide for the early identification of certain metabolic disorders in newborns so that referral and treatment, where appropriate, may be provided. § 6-311

B. **Does it compel screening?** Wholly voluntary. § 6-314(3)

1. **Are there exceptions?** No test will be performed on a newborn over the parent's objection. § 6-314(3)(A)

2. **Does it provide notice to parents and guardians of the right to object?** No test will be performed unless the parent is fully informed of the purpose of testing and is given a reasonable opportunity to object. § 6-314(3)(A)

II. **What does the program screen for and how readily can other tests be added?** Phenylketonuria and hypothyroidism and other metabolic disorders if the mayor specifies by regulation. § 6-313(a)

III. **Does the statute provide for centralization or quality assurance?** A single laboratory is designated (on the advice of the Committee on Metabolic Disorders) which is currently certified by the College of American Pathologists or the U.S. Centers for Disease Control and regularly participates in the appropriate quality control program, or has a federal license under the Clinical Laboratories Improvement Act. § 6-313(b), § 6-316(9)

IV. **Who is responsible . . .**

A. **For each individual screen?** All hospitals. § 6-313(a)

B. **For the program?** The mayor, with the advice of the District of Columbia Committee on Metabolic Disorders. § 6-313(a)

1. **Does the program provide for . . .**

a. **testing** The mayor, on advice of the committee, may specify other tests by regulation. § 6-313(a)

b. **confirming positive result** Follow-up testing should be done when indicated. § 6-313(c)

c. **reporting** All test results shall be reported to the hospital. Positive test results shall be reported to the parents and to a physician designated by the D.C. government. § 6-313(c)

d. **recording** No mention.

e. **treatment** The physician designated by the D.C. government shall assist a parent and her physician in securing appropriate follow-up, testing and treatment when indicated. § 6-313(c)

f. **follow-up** The physician designated by the D.C. government shall assist a parent and her physician in securing appropriate follow-up, testing and treatment when indicated. § 6-313(c)

g. **education** The Committee on Metabolic Disorders shall gather and disseminate information to the public, consult the public, and inform the public on operation of the program. § 6-316(1), (2), and (3)

h. **counseling** No mention. All participants in programs on metabolic disorders will be informed of the nature of risks of participation, the nature and cost of available therapies or maintenance programs for those affected by metabolic disorders, and the possible benefits and risks of such therapies and programs. § 6-314(3)(c)

i. **research** No mention.

j. **other** Carriers of metabolic disorders should not be stigmatized and should not be discriminated against by any person. § 6-314(1)
D.C. policy regarding metabolic disorders should be made with full public knowledge, in light of expert opinion, and should be periodically reviewed to consider changing medical knowledge and ensure full public protection. § 6-314(2) The Committee continuously reevaluates the need for screening, consults experts on the medical, psychological, ethical, social and economic effects of programs for the detection and management of metabolic disorders, and considers the incidence and cost and detection of each metabolic disorder. § 6-316(4) and (7)

2. **Are there confidentiality requirements?** Except for statistical data compiled without reference to the identity of any individual, all information obtained shall be held confidential except for such information as the parent consents to be released. § 6-314(D)

   a. **Who has access?** The parent must be informed of the scope of the information requested to be released and the purpose for releasing such information prior to the release of any confidential information. § 6-314(D)

3. Is a registry established? No mention.

C. For the costs of the program? Laboratory costs of the screening tests shall be borne by the D.C. government. No hospital may charge for the test. § 6-318

V. Are there sanctions to punish non-compliance? No mention.

FLORIDA

I. Is there a statute addressing neonatal genetic screening? Fla. Stat. Ann. § 383.14 (West Supp. 1984). Regulations are set forth in Fla. Admin. Code § 10D-76.01 et seq. They have been updated and expanded in the April 1981 "Guidelines for the Florida Infant Screening Program," published by the Department of Health and Rehabilitative Services.

A. Does it state an objective? To promote the screening of all infants for metabolic, hereditary, and congenital disorders known to result in significant impairment of health or intellect. § 383.14

B. Does it compel screening? Mandatory. § 383.14(1)

1. Are there exceptions? Parents may object with a written statement to the physician or other person whose duty is to report and administer tests. § 383.14(3); Fla. Admin. Code § 10D-76.02

2. Does it provide notice to parents and guardians of the right to object? No mention in the statute. The April 1981 guidelines require advising the parent on the purpose, nature, and procedures of screening before specimen collection. IIa

II. What does the program screen for and how readily can other tests be added? Phenylketonuria and other metabolic, hereditary, or congenital disorders "resulting in significant impairment of health or intellect." § 383.14(1) The regulations provide for screening for phenylketonuria, hypothyroidism, galactosemia, and maple syrup urine disease. § 10D-76.03(1)

III. Does the statute provide for centralization or quality assurance? The availability and quality of the necessary laboratory tests and materials shall be assured by the Department of Health and Rehabilitative Services. § 383.14(2)(a) The regulations in § 10D-76.04 set forth the requirements for approving laboratories including that the laboratory participates in proficiency testing, performs screening on a minimum of 50,000 newborns annually, and reports results in a timely manner.

IV. Who is responsible . . .

A. For each individual screen? According to the regulations, when the birth is in a hospital, the physician is responsible. § 10D-76.03(5) If the birth is outside the facility, the birth attendant is responsible. § 10D-76.03(6)

B. For the program? The Department of Health and Rehabilitative Services, which is empowered to promulgate rules 383.14(2)

1. Does the program provide for . . .

a. testing Testing for phenylketonuria must be done before infant reaches 2 weeks of age. § 383.14(1) The department may promulgate rules regarding method and timing of testing. 383.14(1)
The Infant Screening Advisory Council, appointed by the Secretary of the department, advises the department on conditions for which testing should be established and procedures for collecting, transmitting and recording results from specimens. § 383.14(4) The regulations set forth detailed collection procedures (§ 10D-76.03), including that the specimen be mailed within 24 hours after collection (§ 10D-76.03(3)). The April 1981 guidelines further elaborate on collection procedures. II

b. confirming positive result No mention.

c. reporting Department may promulgate rules for reporting to it. 383.14(1) Forms on which the results are reported shall be furnished by the department to all physicians, public health units, and hospitals. § 383.14(2)(b) According to the regulations a laboratory must report results to the hospital, other birth facility or physician within 7-10 days after receipt of the sample. § 10D-76.06(1) Abnormal tests must be reported immediately to the department, which shall notify by phone the physician (or, if there is none, the county health unit) and designated Regional Genetics Center. The physician or county health unit shall report abnormal results to the parent or guardian. § 10D-76.06(3)

d. recording No mention in the statute. Under the regulations, the laboratories must maintain records for three years or in accordance with department records management procedures. § 10D-76.07(1) The hospitals and other facilities shall report quarterly to the department the number of live births and the number of newborns for whom samples were submitted. § 10D-76.07(3); April 1981 Guidelines VII (c)

e. treatment Where practicable, the department shall supply the necessary dietary treatment products when the products are not otherwise available. § 383.14(2)(e) The April 1981 guidelines provide that physician specialists at the university based Regional Genetic Centers under contract to the department are available to assist in confirming the diagnosis or in providing treatment.

f. **follow-up** The department shall maintain a case registry for the purpose of follow-up services. § 383.14(2)(d)

g. **education** The department shall promote education of the public about the prevention and management of metabolic, hereditary, and congenital disorders. (§ 383.14 (2)(c)

h. **counseling** The department shall promote "the availability of genetic studies and counseling in order that the parents, siblings, and affected infants may benefit from available knowledge of the condition." § 383.14(2)(f)

i. **research** No mention.

j. **other** The Infant Screening Advisory Council provides advice about how the program can be more effectively evaluated, coordinated, and consolidated. § 383.14(4)

2. **Are there confidentiality requirements?** Yes, for the registry. § 383.14(2)(d)

a. **Who has access?** Not specified in the statute. According to the regulations, records will be managed in accordance with the Department's confidentiality requirements. § 10D-76.07(2)

3. **Is a registry established?** A confidential registry of cases shall be maintained by department for purposes of follow-up treatment and epidemiologic studies. § 383.14(2)(d) According to the regulations, it shall include information on every infant diagnosed as having phenylketonuria, neonatal hypothyroidism, galactosemia or maple syrup urine disease to be used only for service delivery and program administration. § 10D-76.07(2)

a. **Is it mandatory?** No mention.

b. **Is it confidential?** Yes. § 383.14(2)(d).

C. **For the costs of the program?** No mention.

V. **Are there sanctions to punish non-compliance?** No mention.

GEORGIA

I. Is there a statute addressing neonatal genetic screening? Ga. Code Ann. §§ 88-1201.1 TO 88-1201.3 (Supp. 1984). Regulations are set forth in Ga. Admin. Comp. ch. 290-5-24.01 et seq. (1983).

A. Does it state an objective? Prevention of mental retardation caused by inherited metabolic disorders. § 88-1201.2(a)

B. Does it compel screening? Mandatory. § 88-1201.2(c)

1. Are there exceptions? Parents may object on religious grounds. § 88-1201.1(a)

2. Does it provide notice to parents and guardians of the right to object? No mention.

II. What does the program screen for and how readily can other tests be added? Phenylketonuria, galactosemia, tyrosinemia, homocystinuria, maple syrup urine disease, hypothyroidism, other such inherited metabolic disorders (§ 88-1201.2(a)), sickle cell anemia and sickle cell trait. § 88-1201.1(b)

III. Does the statute provide for centralization or quality assurance? The Department of Human Resources and appropriate medical centers shall develop a statewide network for medical genetics responsible for the training of personnel in genetics and quality control of laboratory services. § 88-1201.3(a), (b)

IV. Who is responsible . . .

A. For each individual screen? The Department of Human Resources. § 88-1201.2(c) The department regulations provide that, in a hospital birth, the physician shall have responsibility for having the specimen taken before the infant's discharge from the hospital. 290-5-24.02(2) If the birth occurs elsewhere, the person in charge of the facility or the person in attendance shall give written notice to the parents or guardian of the testing requirement and advise where to obtain testing. 290-5-24.02(6)

B. For the program? The Department of Human Resources, which shall promulgate rules and regulations. § 88-1201.2(a)

1. Does the program provide for . . .

a. testing The entire process for screening, retrieval, and diagnosis for must occur within the first three weeks of an infant's life. § 88-

1201.2(b) The regulations provide detailed guidelines for collection of the sample, including that the sample be collected between 48 hours and one week after the child's birth (290-5-24.02(3)), unless the infant is discharged at an earlier time (290-5-24.02(4)). If the infant is tested at the time of an early discharge, a repeat screen must be done before the infant is one week old. 290-5-24.02(4) The sample must be sent to the laboratory on the day of collection. 290-5-24.02(5)

b. **confirming positive result** No mention.

c. **reporting** The regulations provide that the laboratories shall report results to the physician and hospital on the day testing is completed. § 290-5-24.02(7) Additionally, sickle cell results are sent to the health department in the county of the infant's residence. § 290-5-24.02(7) If results are abnormal, the laboratory notifies the appropriate medical facility within 24 hours, which calls the attending physician or, if he or she is unavailable, the parents. § 290-5-24.02(8) The statute provides that it is the responsibility of the examining physician or the department to inform the parents that their child is afflicted. §88-1201.1(b)

d. **recording** No mention in the statutes. According to the regulations, results from testing shall be made a part of the clinical record. § 290-5-24.02(7).

e. **treatment** The department shall provide for initiating and continuing therapy to the extent that state and federal funds are available for such purposes. § 88-1201.2(d)

f. **follow-up** According to the statute, the department shall be responsible for retrieving potentially affected screenees back into the health care system to the extent that state and federal funds are available for such purposes. §88-1201.2(d).

g. **education** No mention.

h. **counseling** Counseling regarding genetically caused disorders shall be provided by a statewide network for medical genetics. §88-1201.3(b) If a child is affected with sickle cell anemia or sickle cell trait, counseling regarding the nature and effects of the disease will be given to the parents. § 88-1201.1(b) Departments and boards of health shall furnish counseling and advice on request, without cost to persons requesting information about sickle cell anemia or sickle cell trait. § 88-1201.1(b) According to the regulations, where a child is affected with sickle cell anemia or sickle cell trait, it is the duty of the attending physician and the county health department to coordinate counseling activities. § 290-5-24.02(9)

i. **research** The department will be responsible for training personnel in research in inborn errors of metabolism. § 88-1201.3(b)

j. **other** "Any person, including but not limited to practitioners of the healing arts, submitting in good-faith reports or data to the department or county boards of health in compliance with the provisions of this Code section shall not be liable for any civil damages therefor." § 31-12-2(b)

2. **Are there confidentiality requirements?** All reports required by the department are deemed confidential and shall not be open to inspection by the public. § 88-1202(a)

   a. **Who has access?** The department may release such reports and data in statistical form or for valid research purposes. § 88-1202(a)

3. **Is a registry established?** No mention.

C. **For the costs of the program?** To the extent state or federal funds are available, the department will provide for retrieving potentially affected screenees back into the health care system; accomplishing specific diagnoses, initiating and continuing therapy; and assessing the program. § 88-1201.2(d)

Treatment for phenylketonuria and sickle cell anemia is available without cost from the department and the county board of health or county department of health. § 88-1201.1(b)

V. **Are there sanctions to punish non-compliance?** No mention.

HAWAII

I. Is there a statute addressing neonatal genetic screening? Hawaii Rev. Stat. Part I § 333-1 (Supp. 1983). Regulations are set forth in the Department of Health Administrative Rules Ch. 142, §§ 11-142-1 through -7 (1981).

A. Does it state an objective? No mention. The regulations are provided to facilitate the detection of metabolic disease and the prevention of mental retardation. § 11-142-1

B. Does it compel screening? Mandatory. § 331-1

1. Are there exceptions? Parents may object on religious grounds. § 333-1 According to the regulations, the parents' written objection must be recorded and the name of the untested child must be submitted to the hereditary metabolic disease register. § 11-142-3(a)(1), (2)

2. Does it provide notice to parents and guardians of the right to object? No mention.

II. What does the program screen for and how readily can other tests be added? Phenylketonuria and hypothyroidism. § 333-1 The regulations pertain only to phenylketonuria. § 11-142-1

III. Does the statute provide for centralization or quality assurance? No mention in the statute. The regulations require that testing for phenylketonuria be performed in the department laboratory or by a laboratory approved in writing by the department. § 11-142-5(a)(2)(A)(B)

IV. Who is responsible . . .

A. For each individual screen? The physician, midwife, or other person attending a newborn. § 333-1

B. For the program? No mention in the statute. The Department of Health has promulgated rules.

1. Does the program provide for . . .

a. testing Not specified in the statute. The regulations outline screening procedures for phenylketonuria. § 11-142-5 Specimens are to be obtained prior to discharge provided infants have been on milk feeding for at least 24 hours. § 11-142-5(b)(1)

b. confirming positive result No mention in the statute. The regulations state that any test revealing 4 mg/100 ml or more of phenylalanine shall be considered positive and presumptive for phenylketonuria. § 11-142-5(d)

c. **reporting** No mention in the statute. According to the regulations, the laboratory must promptly report all presumptively positive tests to the hereditary metabolic disease register and the physician, midwife, or other person responsible for recording the test result. § 11-142-3(C)(1), (2) A physician diagnosing a hereditary metabolic disease must report the results to the hereditary metabolic disease register. § 11-142-3(d) If a child is not tested due to exception on religious grounds, the physician is responsible for recording any written objection and reporting this information to the register. § 11-142-3(b)(1), (2)

d. **recording** No mention in the statute. The physician, midwife, or other person responsible for submitting a specimen is responsible for recording the tests in the medical records of the newborn child. § 11-142-3(a)

e. **treatment** No mention.

f. **follow-up** No mention in the statute. The regulations provide that when a positive result is obtained, the department shall notify the attending physician to obtain an additional blood sample to determine the quantitative level of phenylalanine. § 11-142-5(f)

g. **education** Under another statute, informational and educational services regarding mental retardation may be established by the department for the general public, and for lay and professional groups. § 333-11(2)

h. **counseling** No mention.

i. **research** No mention.

2. **Are there confidentiality requirements?** No mention.

3. **Is a registry established?** No mention in the statute. The regulations require the establishment of a hereditary metabolic disease register (§ 11-142-4) which shall record and maintain a roster of the names of individuals who 1) have been diagnosed as having a specific hereditary metabolic disease or 2) are suspected of having such a disease or 3) have not had a screening test because of religious objections. The register should also include the names of newborn siblings of known diagnosed cases. § 11-142-4 (1) (A)-(D)

a. **Is it mandatory?** Yes.

b. **Is it confidential?** No mention.

C. **For the costs of the program?** No mention.

V. **Are there sanctions to punish non-compliance?** No mention.

IDAHO

I. **Is there a statute addressing neonatal genetic screening?** Idaho Code § 39-909 et seq. (1977). The regulations are set forth in Title 2, Chapter 12, "Rules Governing Procedures and Testing to be Performed on Newborn Infants," 2-12000 et seq. (1980).

A. **Does it state an objective?** No mention.

B. **Does it compel screening?** Mandatory. § 39-909

1. **Are there exceptions?** Parents or guardians belonging to a recognized church or denomination may object on religious grounds. § 39-912

2. **Does it provide notice to parents and guardians of the right to object?** No mention.

II. **What does the program screen for and how readily can other tests be added?** Phenylketonuria and such other tests for preventable diseases as prescribed by the state board of health and welfare. § 39-909 Under its regulations, the department targets "[g]enetic and infectious diseases affecting the newborn population which may cause developmental disabilities of various types [and] are amenable to early detection by available testing procedures." § 2-12002.06

III. **Does the statute provide for centralization or quality assurance?** No mention in the statutes. The regulations indicate that the Idaho Department of Health and Welfare Central Laboratory does testing (§ 2-12105.02), but also indicate that other "approved laboratories" may provide testing (2-12105.03).

IV. **Who is responsible . . .**

A. **For each individual screen?** The administrative officer or other person in charge of each hospital or other institution caring for newborn infants and the person responsible for the registration of the birth of such infant. § 39-909 The regulations spell out further this individual's responsibilities. The administrator must assure inter alia that specimens are adequate and are forwarded within 24 hours to the designated laboratory, that a record is maintained on all specimens collected, and that the birth certificate reflects that the specimen has been collected. § 2-12105.01

B. **For the program?** The director of the Department of Health and Welfare. § 39-910

1. **Does the program provide for . . .**

a. **testing** The director of the department shall prescribe what tests in addition to phenylketonuria shall be made (§ 39-910(2)) and to publish rules prescribing the time and manner of those tests. § 39-910(3) Extensive guidelines for testing are set forth in the regulations (§ 2-12100), including that the newborn's specimen be collected on the day of discharge from the institution where initial newborn care was rendered (§ 2-12100.02(a)), or no later than the fifth day of life if the newborn is receiving domiciliary care in the institution (§ 2-12100.02(c)). In the event of a transfer to another institution the test shall be performed prior to the discharge from the receiving institution. § 12100.02(b). If the infant is born outside of an institution and is not subsequently admitted to one for newborn care, the person registering the birth must cause the test to be administered before the fifth day of the infant's life. § 2-12100.02(d)

b. **confirming positive result** No mention in the statutes. In the case of an abnormal test result, the regulations require the central laboratory to immediately request a second specimen for follow-up testing (§ 2-12105.02(c)) and to provide this service (§ 2-12105.02(e)). If an approved laboratory has an abnormal result, the department must be notified immediately. § 2-12105.03(b)

c. **reporting** The person administering the test shall report the results as required by the state board. § 39-909 The regulations require that the Idaho central laboratory send to the hospital or physician responsible for the collection of the specimen, a report on each specimen tested (§ 2-12105.02(b)) and makes the same requirement for "approved laboratories" (§ 2-12105.03(b)). Approved laboratories must submit a monthly report to the Department of Health and Welfare, Bureau of Child Health, indicating the total number of infants tested § 2-12105.03(e).

d. **recording** No mention in the statutes. The regulations require that the central laboratory shall keep a permanent record of test results (§ 2-12105.02(d)) and that alternative laboratories shall also keep such a record (§ 2-12105.03 (f)).

e. **treatment** The director will supervise local health agencies in treatment and cure of affected infants. § 39-910(5)

f. **follow-up** No mention in the statutes.

g. **education** The director will disseminate information and advice to the public concerning the dangers and effect of phenylketonuria and other preventable diseases and their detection and treatment. § 39-910(6) Copies of the act and rules promulgated will be furnished to physicians, hospitals, or other institutions or persons required to administer tests. § 39-910(4)

h. **counseling** No mention.

i. **research** No mention.

2. **Are there confidentiality requirements?** No mention.

3. **Is a registry established?** The director will maintain a record of all infants with phenylketonuria or other preventable diseases. § 39-910(5)

a. **Is it mandatory?** No mention.

b. **Is it confidential?** No mention.

C. **For the costs of the program?**

No mention in the statutes. The regulations provide that the hospital may assess a suitable charge for collection of the sample. § 2-12105.01(d)

V. **Are there sanctions to punish non-compliance?** Violation is a misdemeanor. § 39-911

ILLINOIS

I. **Is there a statute addressing neonatal genetic screening?** Ill. Ann. Stat. ch. 111½ § 4903 et seq. (Smith-Hurd 1983), as amended by P.A. 83-87 (1983). The regulations are set forth in Illinois Department of Public Health "Rules and Regulations for Prevention of Mental Retardation from Phenylketonuria and Primary Hypothyroidism," Ill. Admin. Reg. § 661.1 et seq. (1981).

A. **Does it state an objective?** To prevent mental retardation resulting from the metabolic disease in early infancy. § 4904 (a)

B. **Does it compel screening?** Mandatory. § 4903

1. **Are there exceptions?** Parents may object on religious grounds by presenting a written statement to the physician or other person required to administer and report the tests. § 4905 Under the regulations, that written refusal must be sent to the State Division of Family Health. § 661.7

2. **Does it provide notice to parents and guardians of the right to object?** No mention.

II. **What does the program screen for and how readily can other tests be added?** Phenylketonuria, hypothyroidism, galactosemia, and other metabolic diseases as the department may deem necessary. § 4903

III. **Does the statute provide for centralization or quality assurance?** All specimens collected will be submitted to the nearest designated Department of Public Health Laboratory, but other licensed medical facilities may collect additional specimens for testing for metabolic or neonatal diseases. § 4904(e) The regulations require that all samples be sent to the Metabolic Diseases Section of the Illinois Department of Public Health Division of Laboratories. § 661.2

IV. **Who is responsible . . .**

A. **For each individual screen?** Physician or other person. § 4905 The regulations provide that the attending physician has responsibility but that, under certain circumstances, he may delegate the responsibility to the hospital administrator or his or her designee. § 661.2 If there is no physician in attendance, the physician caring for the infant during the first month of life has responsibility for seeing that the tests are done. § 661.2. If there is no physician's care during that period, the parents have responsibility. § 661.2

B. **For the program?** The Department of Public Health, which shall promulgate and enforce rules and regulations. § 4903

1. **Does the program provide for . . .**

   a. **testing** The department shall designate tests for other metabolic diseases as deemed necessary. § 4903 The regulations provide for how the tests should be done and interpreted. §§ 661.3, 661.4 They provide that all tests shall be performed within 10 days of collection of the blood sample. § 661.3(e)

   b. **confirming positive result** No mention in the statute. The regulations provide for repeat testing. § 661.4

   c. **reporting** The department may mandate reporting of the results of all tests to the Illinois Dept. of Public Health. § 4903 Under the regulations, hospitals providing screening shall report abnormal results to the Department of Public Health immediately by telephone. § 661.5(b)

   d. **recording** No mention.

   e. **treatment** The department shall supply the necessary treatment product where practicable for diagnosed cases for as long as medically indicated, when the product is not available through other state agencies. § 4904(c) Under the regulations, when positive results are reported, the names of designated pediatric consultants are given to the physicians. § 661.6 The regulations also describe the type of treatment that should be undertaken. § 661.6 The department will arrange for or provide public health nursing, nutrition and social services and clinical consultation as indicated. § 4904(d)

   f. **follow-up** A registry will be maintained for follow-up services to prevent mental retardation. § 4904(b), § 661.6 (regulations)

   g. **education** The department shall educate physicians, hospitals, public health nurses, and the public about the nature of metabolic diseases and examinations for the detection of the diseases in early infancy. § 4904(a)

   h. **counseling** The department shall arrange for social services and clinical consultation as indicated. § 4904(d)

   i. **research** No mention.

2. **Are there confidentiality requirements?** No mention.

3. **Is a registry established?** The department maintains a registry of cases including information of importance for follow-up. § 4904(b), § 661.6 (regulations)

a. **Is it mandatory?** No mention.

b. **Is it confidential?** No mention.

C. **For the costs of the program?** Treatment and public health nursing, nutrition, social services and clinical consultation will be provided when necessary. § 4904(c)(d) The department may develop a reasonable fee structure and may levy fees according to such structure to cover the cost of providing this testing service. Fees collected from the provision of this testing service shall be placed in a special fund in the State Treasury, hereafter known as the Metabolic Screening and Treatment Fund. Other State and federal funds for expenses related to metabolic screening, follow-up and treatment programs may also be placed in such Fund. Moneys shall be appropriated from such Fund to the Department of Public Health solely for the purposes of providing metabolic screening, follow-up and treatment programs. § 4904(e)

V. **Are there sanctions to punish non-compliance?** Any person violating the provisions of § 4904(e) requiring that specimens be sent to the nearest designated Department of Public Health laboratory is guilty of a petty offense.

INDIANA

I. **Is there a statute addressing neonatal genetic screening?** Ind. Code Ann. § 16-8-6-1 et seq. (Burns 1983). The State Board of Health has adopted "Newborn Screening Program for Phenylketonuria and Hypothyroidism: Guidelines" (July 1982).

A. **Does it state an objective?** To prevent mental retardation which results from inborn errors of metabolism. § 16-8-6-1

B. **Does it compel screening?** Mandatory. § 16-8-6-1

1. **Are there exceptions?** Parent may object in writing on religious grounds. § 16-8-6-1 The guidelines require screening but make no note of any exceptions. p. 3

2. **Does it provide notice to parents and guardians of the right to object?** No mention.

II. **What does the program screen for and how readily can other tests be added?** Phenylketonuria, hypothyroidism, and other inborn errors of metabolism. § 16-8-6-1

III. **Does the statute provide for centralization or quality assurance?** The state Board of Health shall designate one or more laboratories to test for hypothyroidism or other inborn errors of metabolism. The laboratories may test for phenylketonuria, but other facilities are not prevented from testing for phenylketonuria. § 16-8-6-6(a) The state Board of Health shall promulgate rules and regulations to insure quality testing procedures at the designated laboratories. § 16-8-6-7(2) The guidelines specify the requirements for designated laboratories and list various proficiency testing programs in which laboratories may participate. pp. 4, 5 They also state that "[o]ptimally, neonatal screening should be part of an integrated program with coordination of testing retrieval, diagnosis, treatment and follow-up of treatment" and specify the names of doctors available for consultative assistance. p. 4

IV. **Who is responsible . . .**

A. **For each individual screen?** Each hospital and physician is responsible for obtaining a specimen from every infant born under their care, and to cause that sample to be transported to a designated laboratory. § 16-8-6-6(b)

B. **For the program?** The state Board of Health, which shall promulgate rules and regulations. § 16-8-6-7

1. **Does the program provide for . . .**

a. testing The state Board of Health, with the advice of medical authorities, determines and requests appropriate tests to be used to detect phenylketonuria. § 16-8-6-3 The state Board of Health shall promulgate rules and regulations to insure proper and timely sample collection and transportation. § 16-8-6-7(1) The guidelines state that 1) full term infants having had protein feeding should have a specimen taken at 3-5 days of age; 2) if discharged before 3 days a sample should be taken at the time of discharge and a second specimen obtained at the age of 5 to 14 days; 3) premature infants should be tested at 6 to 14 days after birth. p. 3

b. confirming positive result No mention in the statute. The guidelines require that an abnormal result in testing for hypothyroidism must be followed up with a filter paper thyroid-stimulating hormone assay on the same blood sample and that diagnosis must be confirmed by serum hormone determinations. With respect to phenylketonuria testing, "an elevated phenylalanine concentration must be followed up by an accurate repeat determination on a serum specimen" p. 3

c. reporting The board shall provide forms for reporting phenylketonuria results to it. The board shall report findings on the extent of such testing to all hospitals, physicians, and other groups interested in child welfare. § 16-8-6-5 The Board of Health will promulgate rules and regulations to insure uniform reporting procedures. § 16-8-6-7(3) The guidelines describe reporting procedures and provide samples of reporting forms. There is very little if any information on the responsibility of reporting to families. However, sample letters are included that may be utilized to notify the physician and/or the parents if results are abnormal. Each hospital must maintain a "Newborn Screening Log" which includes information such as the results of testing, the name of the physician notified about results, an indication of whether or not the family was notified, and any information about confirmatory tests on abnormal results.

The hospital shall make quarterly reports to the state board. Each diagnosed case of phenylketonuria or congenital hypothyroidism must be reported to the Maternal and Child Health Division. p. 6

d. recording No mention in the statute. The guidelines state that hospitals are to keep a newborn screening log. p. 6

e. treatment No mention.

f. **follow-up** No mention in the statute. The guidelines state that confirmatory tests must be performed. p. 3

g. **education** The state Board of Health shall institute and carry on an intensive educational program among physicians, hospitals, public health nurses and the public about the nature and detection of inborn errors of metabolism. § 16-8-6-2

h. **counseling** No mention.

i. **research** No mention.

j. **other** The state board of health and all local boards of health shall encourage and promote the development of plans and procedures for the detection of phenylketonuria in all local health jurisdictions. § 16-8-6-4 The guidelines require that "The screening test and all follow-up confirmatory and diagnostic studies must be accomplished early enough so that therapy, when indicated, can be initiated no later than 21 days of age." p. 3

2. **Are there confidentiality requirements?** No mention.

3. **Is a registry established?** No mention.

C. **For the costs of the program?** No mention.

V. **Are there sanctions to punish non-compliance?** No mention.

IOWA

I. **Is there a statute addressing neonatal genetic screening?** Iowa Code Ann. § 136A.1 et seq. (West Supp. 1984-85). The regulations are set forth in Iowa Admin. Code § 470-4.1 (136A) et seq.

A. **Does it state an objective?** To discover genetic birth defects and related diseases and to prevent or treat the defects or diseases. § 136A.1

B. **Does it compel screening?** Under the regulations, screening is mandatory. § 470-4.1 (136A)

1. **Are there exceptions?** Under the regulations, parental refusal shall be documented in writing and become part of the medical record. § 470-4.2 (136A)

2. **Does it provide notice to parents and guardians of the right to object?** No mention in the statute. Under the regulations, "[p]arents or guardians shall be informed of the type of specimen, how it is obtained, the nature of the diseases being screened, and the consequences of treatment and nontreatment." § 470-4.2(136A)

II. **What does the program screen for and how readily can other tests be added?** Genetic and metabolic disorders. § 136A.2A. Under the regulations, newborn screening shall include testing for hypothyroidism, phenylketonuria, galactosemia, and branched chain ketoaciduria. § 470-4.1 (136A)

III. **Does the statute provide for centralization or quality assurance?** The statute establishes a birth defects institute "to develop and administer genetic and metabolic screening programs." § 136A.2 The institute may develop specifications for a central laboratory. § 136A.3(4) According to the regulations, a central laboratory shall be designated by the Birth Defects Institute (§ 470-4.5 (136A)) and that laboratory shall employ a mechanism that ensures retesting of all inappropriate specimens (§ 470-4.5(1)(136A)). The central laboratory is required to have a written quality assurance plan § 470-4.5(6)(136A). The Birth Defects Institute in collaboration with the central laboratory designates a consulting physician to interpret the test results and consult with the attending physician. § 470-4.5(5)(136A)

IV. **Who is responsible . . .**

A. For each individual screen? No mention in the statute. Under the regulations, the attending physician is responsible. § 470-4.2(136A). If a birth occurs that is not attended by a health professional, the local registrar upon registering the birth certificate, shall inform the parents of the need for screening and where the tests shall be done. § 470-4.4(136A)

B. For the program? The Birth Defects Institute established within the State Department of Health. § 136A.2

1. Does the program provide for . . .

a. testing The regulations provide extensive guidelines for the time the sample should be drawn (§ 470-4.3A(136A) and § 470-4.3B(136A)) and provide that the laboratory shall test specimens within 24 hours of receipt (§ 470-4.5(1)(136A)). The central laboratory provides specimen collection forms and other materials to hospitals and birthing facilities. § 470-4.5(7)(136A)

b. confirming positive result No mention.

c. reporting No mention in the statute. Under the regulations, presumptive positive results are phoned immediately to the physician and Birth Defects Institute, followed within 24 hours by written reports to the physician, Birth Defects Institute and birthing facility. § 470-4.5(2)(136A) Also, the central laboratory makes monthly, quarterly, and annual reports to the Birth Defects Institute. § 470-4.5(4)(136A)

d. recording No mention in the statute.

e. treatment No mention.

f. follow-up No mention.

g. education The Birth Defects Institute shall publish their results and surveys for the benefit of the public health and collate such publications for distribution to scientific organizations and qualified scientists and physicians. (§ 136A.3(2)) The Institute shall implement programs of education and training of medical students, physicians, nurses, scientists and technicians in the causes, methods of treatment, prevention and cure of birth defects. (§ 136A.3(5)) It shall also implement public educational programs to inform persons of the importance of genetic screening and of the various opportunities available. (§ 136A.3(6)) Under the regulations, the central laboratory "shall make educational services concerning specimen collection procedures available to hospitals and other birthing facilities." (§ 470-4.5(3)(136A))

h. **counseling** The Birth Defects Institute shall conduct and support clinical counseling services in medical facilities. § 136A.3(7)

i. **research** The Birth Defects Institute is empowered to conduct investigations and research about the causes, mortality, methods of treatment, prevention, and cure of birth defects and related diseases. § 136A.2, § 136A.3(1)

j. **other** The Birth Defects Institute shall assume responsibility for development and implementation of screening and educational programs for sickle cell anemia and other genetic blood disorders. (§ 136A.2) All state, district, county, and city health or welfare agencies shall co-operate and participate in the implementation of the policy of testing for genetic disorders and birth defects. (§ 136A.6)

2. **Are there confidentiality requirements?** No mention except with respect to registry.

   a. **Who has access?** No mention.

3. **Is a registry established?** The Birth Defects Institute may maintain a central registry to collect and store report data to facilitate the compiling of statistical information on the causes, treatment, prevention, and cure of genetic disorders and birth defects. § 136A.6

   a. **Is it mandatory?** No. § 136A.6

   b. **Is it confidential?** Identifying information shall remain confidential. § 136A.6

C. **For the costs of the program?** Clinical counseling services will be supported by the Birth Defects Institute. § 136A.3(7) In developing laboratory specifications, the institute is to take into account the test costs to the financially responsible private parties and to the state. § 136A.3(4) Under the regulations, the central laboratory acts as fiscal agent for the program charges. § 470-4.5(8)(136A)

V. **Are there sanctions to punish non-compliance?** No mention.

KANSAS

I. **Is there a statute addressing neonatal genetic screening?** Kan. Stat. Ann. § 65-180 et seq. (1980).

   A. **Does it state an objective?** No mention.

   B. **Does it compel screening?** Mandatory. § 65-181

      1. **Are there exceptions?** Parents may object on religious grounds. § 65-182

      2. **Does it provide notice to parents and guardians of the right to object?** No mention.

II. **What does the program screen for and how readily can other tests be added?** Phenylketonuria, congenital hypothyroidism and other such diseases which may detected by the same procedures. § 65-181

III. **Does the statute provide for centralization or quality assurance?** No mention.

IV. **Who is responsible . . .**

   A. **For each individual screen?** The attending physician or the administrative officer or other person in charge of each institution caring for infants 28 days or less of age. § 65-181

   B. **For the program?** The Secretary of Health and Environment § 65-180

      1. **Does the program provide for . . .**

         a. **testing** The secretary will provide for screening. § 65-180(b) Testing shall be performed at such times and in such manner as may be prescribed by the secretary. § 65-181

         b. **confirming positive result** No mention.

         c. **reporting** Every physician having an affected patient shall report the case to the secretary on forms provided. § 65-183 A Kansas Bureau of Maternal and Child Health publication describes the method of reporting.

         d. **recording** Recording results shall be performed at such times and in such manner as prescribed by the secretary. § 65-181

         e. **treatment** The secretary will provide the necessary treatment product for diagnosed cases for as long as medically indicated when the product is not available through other state agencies. § 65-180(d)

f. **follow-up** Information will be maintained for follow-up services to prevent mental retardation. § 65-180(c)

g. **education** The secretary will carry on an extensive education program among physicians, hospitals, public health nurses and the public concerning congenital hypothyroidism and phenylketonuria, including information about the nature of such conditions and examinations for early detection. § 65-180(a)

h. **counseling** No mention.

i. **research** No mention.

2. **Are there confidentiality requirements?** No mention.

3. **Is a registry established?** The secretary shall maintain a registry of cases including information for follow-up services to prevent mental retardation. § 65-180(c)

a. **Is it mandatory?** No mention.

b. **Is it confidential?** No mention.

C. **For the costs of the program?** Screenings and tests made by the office of laboratory services shall be made without charge. § 65-180(b)

V. **Are there sanctions to punish non-compliance?** No mention.

KENTUCKY

I. **Is there a statute addressing neonatal genetic screening?** Ky. Rev. Stat. § 214.155 (1982). The regulations are set forth in 902 Ky. Admin. Regs. 4:030.

A. **Does it state an objective?** No mention.

B. **Does it compel screening?** Mandatory. § 214.155(1), § 4:030(1) (regulations)

1. **Are there exceptions?** Parents belonging to a nationally recognized and established church or religious denomination may object in writing on religious grounds. § 214.155(2)

2. **Does it provide notice to parents and guardians of the right to object?** No mention.

II. **What does the program screen for and how readily can other tests be added?** Phenylketonuria and other inborn errors of metabolism. § 214.155(1) Under the regulations screening shall include testing for phenylketonuria, galactosemia and hypothyroidism. 4:030(1)

III. **Does the statute provide for centralization or quality assurance?** No mention in the statute. Under the regulations, hospitals and institutions may submit blood samples to the Department for Human Resources, Bureau for Health Services, Laboratory Services. If a hospital conducts its own tests, the department must be notified and the laboratory procedures approved. A private laboratory is required by the department to demonstrate its proficiency. 4:030(2)

IV. **Who is responsible . . .**

A. **For each individual screen?** The administrative officer or other persons in charge of each institution caring for infants twenty-eight days or less of age and the person required to register the child's birth. § 214.155(1) § 4:030(1) (regulations)

B. **For the program?** The Secretary for Human Resources, who may promulgate rules and regulations. § 214.155(1)

1. **Does the program provide for . . .**

a. **testing** Testing shall be performed at such times and in such manner as prescribed by the secretary. § 214.155(1)

b. **confirming positive result** No mention.

c. **reporting** Positive results shall be reported to the Department for Health Services no later than two weeks after the date of testing. § 214.155(1) Under the regulations positive results must be reported within 24 hours to the department and to the attending physician. 4:030(2)

d. **recording** Recording of the results of such tests shall be performed at such times and in such places as prescribed by the secretary. § 214.155(1)

e. **treatment** No mention.

f. **follow-up** No mention.

g. **education** No mention.

h. **counseling** No mention.

i. **research** No mention.

2. **Are there confidentiality requirements?** No mention.

3. **Is a registry established?** No mention.

C. **For the costs of the program?** The secretary shall establish and collect fees to cover the cost of analyzing the samples. (§ 214-155(1)) Under the regulations, tests performed at the state laboratory are performed without charge. § 4:030(2)

V. **Are there sanctions to punish non-compliance?** No mention.

LOUISIANA

I. Is there a statute addressing neonatal genetic screening? La. Rev. Stat. Ann. § 40.1299 et seq. (West Supp. 1984). The Department of Health and Human Resources has provided "Guidelines: Neonatal Screening Programs."

- **A. Does it state an objective?** To combat mental retardation in children suffering from a genetic defect. § 1299
- **B. Does it compel screening?** Mandatory. § 1299.1
  1. **Are there exceptions?** Parental objection. § 1299.1
  2. **Does it provide notice to parents and guardians of the right to object?** No mention in the statutes. The guidelines state that families need to be educated at the time of discharge or specimen collection about the importance of neonatal screening. § II(A) However, the sample brochure provided in the guidelines says screening is required by law, but does not indicate parents may object. § II(N)(1)

II. What does the program screen for and how readily can other tests be added? Sickle cell anemia, phenylketonuria, congenital hypothyroidism, galactosemia, maple syrup urine disease, homocystinuria, and tyrosinemia. § 1299.1 The guidelines provide for phenylketonuria testing of pregnant women who are mentally retarded or have a family history of phenylketonuria (§ III (D)(1)) and for such testing of mentally retarded individuals or patients referred to Handicapped Children's Program Clinics for whom there is no record of such a test (§ III (D)(2) and (3)), family members of a known case of phenylketonuria or familial mental retardation (§ III D(3)), or infants beyond the neonatal period for whom there is no definitive record of a phenylketonuria screen (§ III D(3)).

III. Does the statute provide for centralization or quality assurance? The Department of Health and Human Resources shall establish and maintain a diagnostic laboratory to develop tests. § 1299 The guidelines provide that the department is to maintain a laboratory. § II A

IV. Who is responsible . . .

- **A. For each individual screen?** The physician attending a newborn or person attending a newborn not attended by a physician. § 1299.1

B. For the program? The Department of Health and Human Resources, which may adopt rules and regulations. § 1299

1. Does the program provide for . . .

a. testing The department approves tests to be administered. § 1299.1 The guidelines require testing within the first three to seven days of life (§ II A) and provide detailed descriptions of how testing should be undertaken (§§ II B, C, D and III C).

b. confirming positive result Positive tests shall be confirmed. § 1299.1

c. reporting If any tests are positive, the attending physician shall notify the department. § 1299.1 A sample report form is provided in the guidelines. § II B phenylketonuria reporting is covered in the guidelines. § III C(1)(b)

d. recording No mention in the statute. The guidelines provide that the central laboratory maintain a permanent record of all positive tests. § III C(1)(b).

e. treatment The department, in cooperation with the attending physician, will provide for the continued medical care, dietary, and other related needs of the affected children. § 1299.1 Treatments are described in the guidelines. §§ II A, III A For phenylketonuria, the department (in cooperation with other state agencies and attending physicians) offers "medical consultation for definitive diagnoses, nutrition counseling, Lofenalac and Phenyl-Free formulas, and Maternal and Child Health nursing follow-up. . . ." § III B,E The guidelines provide for monitoring plasma levels in phenylketonuria patients. § III C(3) They also provide that a phenylketonuria child "should be evaluated at regular intervals as recommended by the attending physician or the consultant psychologist." § III E(5)

f. follow-up All positive tests will be followed-up by the department and when confirmed, the department shall inform either the physician or the parents or both that services and facilities are available. § 1299.1 The guidelines detail the follow-up requirements for inadequate samples (§ II E), no-shows (§ II F), non-receipt of initial reports (§ II G), positive results (§ II H), non-receipt of repeats (§ II I), and negative and positive phenylketonuria results. III C(1)(c) and (2)

g. education No mention in the statute. The guidelines states that "[f]amilies need to be educated at the time of discharge or at specimen collection as to the importance of neonatal screening for their child. . . ." and provide an example brochure. § II A The guidelines also discuss the availability of a slide and tape presentation as part of a training session for those who collect specimens. § II N(7).

h. counseling No mention.

i. research The Department laboratory will conduct experiments, projects, and other undertakings as may be necessary to develop tests or for developing ways to prevent or treat the enumerated diseases. § 1299

j. other The various boards, commissions, departments and agencies of the state and of the parishes, municipalities and other political subdivisions capable of assisting or having services or facilities for assisting the Department of Health and Human Resources in carrying out any program established may cooperate with the Department and furnish any such services or facilities in aid of any such program. § 1299.2

2. Are there confidentiality requirements? No mention.

3. Is a registry established? No mention in the statute. The guidelines provide for a central registry of phenylketonuria patients. § III F

a. Is it mandatory? No mention.

b. Is it confidential? No mention.

C. For the costs of the program? Services and facilities shall be made available to the extent needed by the family and physician. § 1299.1 The guidelines detail procedures instituted to facilitate third party collections for the provision of Lofenalac, Phenyl-Free and Maple Syrup Urine Diet Powder. § III E(2)(b)

V. Are there sanctions to punish non-compliance? No mention.

MAINE

I. Is there a statute addressing neonatal genetic screening? Me. Rev. Stat. Ann. tit. 22, § 1522 (1980). The State Department of Human Services has adopted "Rules and Regulations Relating to Testing Newborn Infants for Detection of Causes of Mental Retardation" 1-7.

A. Does it state an objective? No mention.

B. Does it compel screening? The Department of Human Services is authorized to require testing. § 1522

1. Are there exceptions? Parents may object on religious grounds. § 1522 The regulations provide that the objection shall be in writing and made part of the medical record of the infant. § 2

2. Does it provide notice to parents and guardians of the right to object? No mention.

II. What does the program screen for and how readily can other tests be added? Metabolic abnormalities which may be expected to result in subsequent mental deficiencies. § 1522 The regulations provide that samples shall be tested for phenylketonuria, homocystinuria, galactosemia, maple syrup urine disease, hypothyroidism and other diseases as cost effective testing procedures become available. § 3

III. Does the statute provide for centralization or quality assurance? The Department may offer consultation, training and evaluation services to testing facilities. § 1522 Under the regulations, specimens shall be collected with kits provided by the Department of Human Services, Public Health Laboratory and shall be forwarded to the Laboratory daily with a corresponding list of names. § 6

IV. Who is responsible . . .

A. For each individual screen? The department may require hospitals, maternity homes, and other maternity services to test. § 1522 The regulations make responsible the hospital, birthing center or baby deliverer. § 1

B. For the program? The Department of Human Services, which shall promulgate rules and regulations. § 1522

1. Does the program provide for . . .

a. testing The Department shall approve testing methods, materials, procedure and testing sequences. § 1522 The regulations provide guidelines for the timing of testing (§§ 4 and 5) and require that specimens should be shipped daily to the Department of Human Services, Public Health Laboratory. § 6 The department provides the testing kits. § 6

b. **confirming positive result** No mention.

c. **reporting** Reports may be required to be submitted to the department. § 1522 Under the regulations, the list of names sent with specimen forms shall be used as a report form to the hospital, birthing center or baby deliverer with the results of the tests. § 6

d. **recording** Records may be required to be submitted to the department. § 1522

e. **treatment** No mention.

f. **follow-up** No mention.

g. **education** No mention.

h. **counseling** No mention.

i. **research** No mention.

2. **Are there confidentiality requirements?** No mention.

3. **Is a registry established?** No mention.

C. **For the costs of the program?** No mention.

V. **Are there sanctions to punish non-compliance?** No mention in the statute. Failure to comply with the regulations subjects the person to civil and criminal penalties. § 7

MARYLAND

I. **Is there a statute addressing neonatal genetic screening?** Md. Pub. Health Code Ann. § 13-101 to -111 (1982 and Supp. 1984). The regulations are set forth in Md. Admin. Code § 10.38 (1975).

A. **Does it state an objective?** To alleviate the disability of some hereditary disorders and further the understanding of and accumulation of medical knowledge about other hereditary disorders that may lead to their eventual alleviation or care. § 13-102(3) (1982)

B. **Does it compel screening?** Participation in a hereditary disorder program should be wholly voluntary. § 13-102(10) (1982) and § 13-109(f) (1982)

1. **Are there exceptions?** Not applicable.

2. **Does it provide notice to parents and guardians of the right to object?** Testing of an individual for a hereditary disorder is prohibited unless the parent or guardian (i) is informed fully of the purpose of the test and the nature and consequences of being a carrier of a hereditary disorder; (ii) is given a reasonable opportunity to object; and (iii) does not object. § 13-109(e)(2) (1982) The process for obtaining consent is set forth in the regulations. § 10.38.04(C)

II. **What does the program screen for and how readily can other tests be added?** Hereditary disorder (any disorder transmitted through the genetic material DNA). § 13-101 (1982) According to the regulations, this includes phenylketonuria and maple syrup urine disease. § 10.38.02(D)

III. **Does the statute provide for centralization or quality assurance?** No mention in the statute. The regulations provide that tests should be performed by the department or a laboratory approved by the department and the commission. § 10.38.07(A) The department furnishes materials for testing. § 10.38.07(B)

IV. **Who is responsible . . .**

A. **For each individual screen?** No mention in the statute. According to the regulations, it is the duty of the person in charge of the birth facility or his designee. § 10.38.04 If the child is born outside of an institution, it is the responsibility of the person required to file the birth certificate. § 10.38.05.

B. For the program? The State Commission on Hereditary Disorders, which may adopt rules, regulations, and standards (after consulting the public and, where appropriate, experts). § 13-109(a), (b)(1) (1982) The procedures shall be accurate, provide maximum information, be set forth clearly, and be reviewed regularly. § 13-109(d)(1)-(4) (1982)

1. Does the program provide for . . .

a. testing The commission may adopt rules, regulations, and standards for the detection and management of hereditary disorders. § 13-109(a) (1982) The timing of the testing is set forth in the regulations. § 10.38.04(B) A second test is strongly recommended on the child's first visit to the doctor, preferably when the child is between the ages of 1 and 4 weeks. § 10.38.06 The samples must be mailed to the laboratory within 24 hours of collection. § 10.38.07(C)

b. confirming positive result No mention in the statutes. The regulations provide that the department shall disseminate abnormal results to the appropriate institution or individual which shall then alert the parent or guardian of the need for a follow up serum analysis. § 10.38.09(B)

c. reporting Unambiguous diagnostic results are to be made available through a physician or other source of health care to the individual, or the parent or guardian. § 13-109(e)(3) (1982) Under the regulations, within seven days of the receipt of the specimen, the laboratory must report the results to the responsible institution, physician, or local health department. In the case of an institution, the results should be available to the parent on request. § 10.38.07(D) The laboratory director must also notify the designated representative of the Department of any abnormal results within a week of receipt of the specimen. § 10.38.09(A)

d. recording The commission shall establish systems to record information obtained in hereditary disorder programs. § 13-108(2) (1982)

e. treatment Each participant shall be informed of the nature, cost, benefits, and risks of any therapy or maintenance program available for an affected individual. § 13-109(g)(1)(ii) (1982)

f. follow-up No mention in the statute. There are extensive provisions for the follow-up of abnormal results in the regulations, including the recommendation that no treatment be administered until follow-up tests have confirmed the presence of a disorder. § 10.38.09(B).

g. **education** The commission shall gather and give out information to further the public's understanding of hereditary disorders. § 13-108(1) (1982)

h. **counseling** Each participant in a screening program for a hereditary disorder shall have counseling services available that (i) are non-directive, (ii) emphasize informing the individual, (iii) do not require restriction in childbearing. § 13-109(g)(2) (1982) The regulations provide that the counseling services should be available on request. § 10.38.10

i. **research** No mention.

j. **other** The commission may investigate and make any necessary recommendation to end any unjustified discrimination that might result from identification of an individual as a carrier of a hereditary disorder, but this does not affect any right of anyone to seek or have any other redress for this discrimination. § 13-108(4) (1982) Before the commission adopts a rule, regulation, or standard, the incidence of each disorder and the cost of detection and management shall be considered. § 13-109(b)(2) (1982) The commission reports annually to the Governor and General Assembly. § 13-107 (1982) The commission continually reevaluates the need for and the effectiveness of state hereditary disorder programs. § 13-108(3) (1982) The commission rules, regulations, and standards shall provide that each participant in a hereditary disorder program shall be protected from undue physical or mental harm. § 13-109(g)(1)(i) (1982)

2. **Are there confidentiality requirements?** Each person who conducts a hereditary disorder program "shall keep in code and treat as a confidential medical record all information that is gathered in the program and identifies an individual." § 13-109(c) (1982)

   a. **Who has access?** The disclosure of information is not prevented if the person or parent is informed of the scope of information to be released, the purpose of the release, and consents. § 13-109(c)(1) (1982) Subject to the restrictions on disclosure of confidential information, information on the operation of a hereditary disorder program shall be open and freely available to the public. § 13-109(c)(2) (1982)

3. **Is a registry established?** No direct mention in the statutes. Under the regulations, the department shall maintain a register of all children with confirmed diagnoses of a hereditary metabolic disorder. § 10.38.11.

   a. **Is it mandatory?** No mention.

b. Is it confidential? The regulations require that the register shall be treated as confidential medical records. § 10.38.11

C. For the costs of the program? The Secretary shall disburse and collect funds available to the commission. § 13-110(2) (1982) The department shall request the budget support necessary for the commission to carry out its duties. § 13-111 (1982)

V. Are there sanctions to punish non-compliance? No mention.

MASSACHUSETTS

I. **Is there a statute addressing neonatal genetic screening?** Mass. Ann. Laws ch. 111, § 110A (Michie/Law Coop Supp. 1983).

A. **Does it state an objective?** No mention.

B. **Does it compel screening?** Mandatory. § 110A

1. **Are there exceptions?** Parents may object on religious grounds. § 110A

2. **Does it provide notice to parents and guardians of the right to object?** No mention.

II. **What does the program screen for and how readily can other tests be added?** Until June 1, 1986, phenylketonuria, cretinism and such other specifically treatable genetic or biochemical disorders. After June 1, 1986 phenylketonuria, cretenism, tuberous sclerosis and such other specifically treatable genetic or biochemical disorders. § 110A

III. **Does the statute provide for centralization or quality assurance?** No mention.

IV. **Who is responsible . . .**

A. **For each individual screen?** Physician attending a newborn child. § 110A

B. **For the program?** The Commissioner of Public Health, who may convene an advisory committee on newborn screening. § 110A The Department of Public Health shall "make such rules pertaining to such tests as accepted medical practice shall indicate." § 110A.

1. **Does the program provide for . . .**

a. **testing** Tests to be performed as specified by the commissioner. § 110A

b. **confirming positive result** No mention.

c. **reporting** No mention.

d. **recording** No mention.

e. **treatment** No mention.

f. **follow-up** No mention.

g. **education** No mention.

h. **counseling** No mention.

i. **research** No mention.

2. **Are there confidentiality requirements?** No mention.

3. **Is a registry established?** No mention.

C. For the costs of the program? No mention.

V. Are there sanctions to punish non-compliance? No mention.

See also ch. 76 § 15B, which establishes a voluntary screening program for sickle cell anemia, Tay-Sachs, Cooley's anemia, hemophilia and similar disorders. The Department shall furnish necessary laboratory and testing facilities. Provides for health education, post-screening counseling service and treatment of those affected by any blood abnormality as the commissioner deems appropriate or practical. Records shall be confidential and inaccessible to anyone other than the commissioner or his agents or to the local health department conducting the screening program except by parents' permission. Information on results shall be limited to the parents. Otherwise, the results may be used only for collective statistical purposes. This statute may be drafted broadly enough to be an effective mechanism to reach subjects not mentioned in the newborn screening statute.

MICHIGAN

I. **Is there a statute addressing neonatal genetic screening?** Mich. Comp. Laws. Ann. §§ 333.5431, 5439 (West 1980). The regulations are set forth in Mich. Admin. Code R 325.1471-1475 (1966).

A. **Does it state an objective?** No mention.

B. **Does it compel screening?** Mandatory. § 333.5431(1)

1. **Are there exceptions?** No mention.

2. **Does it provide notice to parents and guardians of the right to object?** No mention.

II. **What does the program screen for and how readily can other tests be added?** Phenylketonuria and other handicapping conditions as designated by the department. § 333.5431(1)

III. **Does the statute provide for centralization or quality assurance?** No mention in the statutes. The regulations provide that laboratories are subject to quality control by the department, including testing of unknown control specimens and the inclusion of a control series with certain specified phenylalanine levels with each test plate. R 325.1473(a)(c) and (e).

IV. **Who is responsible . . .**

A. **For each individual screen?** A health professional in charge of a newborn's care or, if none, the health professional in charge at the birth of an infant. § 333.5431(1)

B. **For the program?** The Department of Public Health, which may promulgate rules and regulations. § 333.5439

1. **Does the program provide for . . .**

a. **testing** Type, time, and conditions of tests shall be designated by the department. § 333.5431(1) The approved testing procedure is set forth in R 325.1471-1472. Tests must be performed no later than three days after receipt of specimens. R 325.1473(d) Unsatisfactory specimens must be reported by the laboratory to the responsible physician (R 325.1473(g)), who must then submit a repeat specimen within 72 hours. (R 325.1474)

b. **confirming positive result** When presumptive positive is reported, a second specimen shall be requested to be submitted within 72 hours and therapy shall not be instituted until confirmatory diagnostic testing is reported positive. R.325.1475(1)

c. **reporting** Results of a positive test shall be reported to the infants' parents. § 333.5431(1) According to the regulations, the laboratory must "[r]eport immediately presumptive positive tests by telephone to the responsible physician and by telephone or telegraph to the offices of the state health director." R 325.1473(f) Written reports of tests shall be made to the responsible physician through the agency submitting the specimen. R 325.1475(1)

d. **recording** No mention.

e. **treatment** No mention.

f. **follow-up** No mention.

g. **education** No mention.

h. **counseling** No mention.

i. **research** No mention in the statute. The regulations provide that tests other than the Guthrie test may be used on controlled research conditions upon prior written approval of the state health director. R 325.1471

2. **Are there confidentiality requirements?** No mention.

3. **Is a registry established?** No mention.

C. **For the costs of the program?** No mention in the statute. Under the regulations, the Guthrie test shall be provided without charge by the department to all Michigan physicians and hospitals. R 325.1471

V. **Are there sanctions to punish non-compliance?** Misdemeanor penalties. § 333.5431(2)

MINNESOTA

I. **Is there a statute addressing neonatal genetic screening?** Minn. Stat. Ann. § 144.125 (West Supp. 1983). Regulations are set forth in 7 Minn. Code Agency R. 1.172 (1979).

A. **Does it state an objective?** No mention.

B. **Does it compel screening?** Mandatory. § 144.125

1. **Are there exceptions?** Parents may object on religious grounds. § 144.125

2. **Does it provide notice to parents and guardians of the right to object?** No mention in the statute. Under the regulations it is the administrative officer's or physician's duty to inform parents of the reasons for screening and their right to refuse on religious grounds. R. 1.172 C 1(a)

II. **What does the program screen for and how readily can other tests be added?** Phenylketonuria and other inborn errors of metabolism causing mental retardation as prescribed by the state commissioner of health. § 144.125 The regulations specify screening for phenylketonuria, galactosemia and hypothyroidism. R. 1.172A

III. **Does the statute provide for centralization or quality assurance?** No mention in the statute. The regulations require that specimens be sent to the Minnesota Department of Health laboratory. § 1.127 C 1(d) The department shall develop specimen cards and make them available at no charge to the responsible party. R. 1.172 C 2(a)

IV. **Who is responsible . . .**

A. **For each individual screen?** The administrative officer or other person in charge of each institution caring for infants 28 days or less of age and the person required to register the birth of a child. § 144.125 Under the regulations "responsible party" includes the physician or person operating under his supervision at the birth or if the birth is not attended, one of the parents. R. 1.172 B (4)

B. **For the program?** The State Commissioner of Health, who may promulgate rules and regulations. § 144.125.

1. **Does the program provide for . . .**

a. **testing** Tests shall be performed at such times and in such manner as prescribed by the commissioner. § 144.125 The regulations specify content of specimen forms, responsibilities of the parties, and timing of tests. R. 1.172 C 1

b. confirming positive result No mention.

c. reporting Reporting of results shall be performed at such time and in such manner as prescribed by the commissioner. § 144.125 The regulations require that the department notify the attending physician within 24 hours of a positive test result. R. 1.172 C 2(c) The physician is to report in writing all confirmed cases to the Human Genetics Unit. R. 1.172 C 3(a)

d. recording No mention in the statute. Under the regulations, the responsible party is to record on a permanent record the date the specimen is collected. R. 1.172 C(1)(c) Also, the department is required to maintain a record of all cases of phenylketonuria, galactosemia and hypothyroidism reported to it. R. 1.172 C 2(b).

e. treatment No mention in statute. The regulations require that the department provide consultation on diagnostic and treatment services available. R. 1.172 C 2(c)

f. follow-up No mention.

g. education No mention.

h. counseling No mention.

i. research No mention.

2. Are there confidentiality requirements? No mention.

3. Is a registry established? No mention in the statute. The regulations require that the department maintain a record of all cases. R. 1.172 C 2(b)

a. Is it mandatory? Yes. R. 1.172 C 2(b)

b. Is it confidential? No mention.

C. For the costs of the program? No mention in the statute. The regulations provide that the department shall develop specimen cards and make them available at no charge to the responsible party. R. 1.172 C 2(a)

V. Are there sanctions to punish non-compliance? No mention.

MISSISSIPPI

I. **Is there a statute addressing neonatal genetic screening?** Miss. Code Ann. §§ 41-21-201, 203 (1984).

A. **Does it state an objective?** To combat mental retardation in children suffering from a genetic defect which causes hypothyroidism or phenylketonuria. § 41-21-201

B. **Does it compel screening?** Mandatory after July 1, 1985. § 41-21-203

1. **Are there exceptions?** Religious objection. § 41-21-203

2. **Does it provide notice to parents and guardians of the right to object?** No mention.

II. **What does the program screen for and how readily can other tests be added?** Phenylketonuria and hypothyroidism. § 41-21-203

III. **Does the statute provide for centralization or quality assurance?** No mention.

IV. **Who is responsible . . .**

A. **For each individual screen?** The physician, or if none, the person attending a newborn. § 41-21-203

B. **For the program?** The State Board of Health, which is authorized to promulgate rules and regulations. § 14-21-201

1. **Does the program provide for . . .**

a. **testing** The state Board of Health shall approve tests. § 41-21-203

b. **confirming positive result** The test must be confirmed before state facilities are made available for treatment. § 41-21-203

c. **reporting** No mention.

d. **recording** No mention.

e. **treatment** The services and facilities of the state Board of Health and co-operating agencies shall be made available to the extent needed by the physician. § 41-21-203

f. **follow-up** The state Board of Health shall follow-up all positive tests with the attending physician who notified the board thereof or with the parents of the newborn when notification was made by a person other than a physician. § 41-21-203

g. **education** No mention.

h. **counseling** No mention.

i. **research** No mention.

2. **Are there confidentiality requirements?** No mention.

3. **Is a registry established?** No mention.

C. **For the costs of the program?** No mention.

V. **Are there sanctions to punish non-compliance?** No mention.

MISSOURI

I. **Is there a statute addressing neonatal genetic screening?** Mo. Ann. Stat. § 210.065 (Vernon 1983). Regulations are set forth in Mo. Admin. Code tit. 13, § 50-143.010 (1981).

A. **Does it state an objective?** No mention.

B. **Does it compel screening?** Mandatory. § 210.065.1

1. **Are there exceptions?** Parents may object on religious grounds. § 210.065.4 See also regulations § 50-143.10.

2. **Does it provide notice to parents and guardians of the right to object?** No mention in the statute. The regulations specify that the objection shall be obtained in writing and filed in the office of the attending physician, other health professional, hospital or public health facility, with a copy sent to the Division of Health. § 50-143.010 (2)

II. **What does the program screen for and how readily can other tests be added?** Phenylketonuria and other metabolic defects as are prescribed by the division of health. § 210.065.1 The regulations additionally require primary hypothyroidism testing. § 50-143.010

III. **Does the statute provide for centralization or quality assurance?** No mention in the statute. The regulations state that tests must be performed in the Division of Health Central laboratory or a laboratory approved by the Division of Health. § 50-143.010 (C) Requirements for approval are stated in the rules and include the provisions that laboratories be properly equipped and adequately constructed for testing procedures prescribed by the Division. § 50-143.010 (4) (A) (1-8) The regulations also establish guidelines for quality assurance which include evaluation by the Division of Health central laboratory using sample specimens to test the proficiency of laboratory analysis. § 50-143.010 (4) (B) (1-6) In addition, to be approved, a laboratory must have a director who shall assume responsibility for the accuracy of tests and reports (§ 150-143.010 (4) (A) (2)) and must perform a minimum number of hypothyroid tests per week. (§ 150-143.010 (3) (B) (3)) The regulations also provide for the possibility of using an out-of-state laboratory to process samples if the other state's health officer has approved the laboratory and the other state has rules at least as stringent as those of Missouri. § 50-143.010 (4) (C) (7)

IV. Who is responsible . . .

A. For each individual screen? The parent, guardian or custodian is responsible for the performance of the tests through the physician, midwife, public health facility or hospital. § 210.065.1 According to the regulations it is the responsibility of the attending physician or other health professional to notify parents of their responsibility to have testing performed. § 50-143.010 (1) (B)

B. For the program? The Division of Health, which shall adopt rules. § 210.065.1

1. Does the program provide for . . .

a. testing The Division of Health shall promulgate rules pertaining to the tests. § 210.065.1 According to the regulations, approved test methods and practices include collecting a blood sample between 3 and 5 days after birth provided protein feeding has been initiated for at least 24 hours. § 50-143.010 (3) (A) Special provisions are stated for the collection of specimens from ill or premature infants ((3)(A)(1)), infants who leave the hospital before protein feeding for at least 24 hours ((3)(A)(2)), and infants not born in hospitals or not admitted to hospitals during the neonatal period ((3)(A)(3)). Blood samples must be submitted to the laboratory no later than 72 hours after collection. (3)(A)(4) The regulations additionally specify the testing methodology. § 50-143.010 (3) (B)

b. confirming positive result No mention.

c. reporting All physicians, public health nurses, and hospital administrators shall report the discovery of metabolic defects to the Division of Health. § 210.065.2 The Division shall prescribe and furnish all necessary reporting forms. § 210.065.3 The regulations require that all physicians, hospitals and laboratories conducting tests for phenylketonuria or hypothyroidism shall report all presumptive positive test results and positive screening in writing to the attending physician and the Division of Health within 7 working days of receipt of the sample. § 50-143.010 (5)

d. recording No mention.

e. treatment No mention.

f. follow-up No mention.

g. education The Division of Health shall institute and carry on educational programs about phenylketonuria and other metabolic defects and examinations for detecting them for physicians, hospitals, public health nurses and the general public. § 210.065.3

h. counseling No mention.

i. **research** No mention.

2. **Are there confidentiality requirements?** No mention.

3. **Is a registry established?** No mention.

C. **For the costs of the program?** No mention.

V. **Are there sanctions to punish non-compliance?** The parents of any child who fail to have the test(s) administered after notice of the requirement by the physician shall be guilty of a misdemeanor, unless they object on religious grounds. §§ 210.065.5, 210.065.4

MONTANA

I. Is there a statute addressing neonatal genetic screening? Mont. Code Ann. § 50-19-201 et seq. (1983). Regulations are set forth in Mont. Admin. Code 16-2.18 (6)-S1820.

A. Does it state an objective? To detect inborn metabolic errors. § 50-19-203(1)

B. Does it compel screening? Mandatory. § 50-19-203(1)

1. Are there exceptions? No mention.

2. Does it provide notice to parents and guardians of the right to object? No mention.

II. What does the program screen for and how readily can other tests be added? Those inborn errors of metabolism that the department's rules cover. § 50-19-203(1) The rules provide for testing for inborn errors of metabolism, including phenylketonuria and tests for detection of other amino acidopathies. 16-2.18(6)-S1820 (1)

III. Does the statute provide for centralization or quality assurance? Tests shall be done by a laboratory approved by the department or by the laboratory of the department. § 50-19-203(2) See also regulations 16-2.18(6)-S1820 (2) (3)

IV. Who is responsible . . .

A. For each individual screen? A person in charge of the facility where the infant is born or cared for, or a person responsible for the registration of birth. § 50-19-203(1); 16-2.18 (6)-S1820 (1) (regulations) According to the regulations, when an infant is born outside a health care facility and not subsequently admitted for newborn care, the person required to register the birth shall cause the test to be administered unless medically contraindicated. 16-2.18(6)-S1820(8)

B. For the program? The Department of Health and Environmental Sciences, which may adopt rules. § 50-19-202

1. Does the program provide for . . .

a. testing The department shall determine which tests are required. § 50-19-203(1) According to the regulations specimens should be collected on the third day of life or 48 hours following ingestion of milk but not later than the 14th day of life. 16-2.18(6)-S1820(5) The regulations specify special provisions for collecting specimens from infants discharged before the third day of life, premature infants and infants transferred to other facilities. 16-2.18(6)-S1820(5), (6), (7)

b. **confirming positive result** No mention in the statute. The regulations require that a positive or suspicious initial test must be followed by a second test. If the second test is positive, a blood sample will be sent to the laboratory for a quantitative analysis. 16-2.18(6)-S1820(9)

c. **reporting** The department may determine the procedures for advising the physician, parents, or legal guardian of test results. § 50-19-204(2) The regulations require that the laboratory report all positive or suspicious test results to the department within 48 hours after drawing the blood and performing the test. 16-2-18(6)-S1820(3)

d. **recording** No mention in the statute. The regulations require that the administrator of the responsible hospital and the person required to register the birth of a child must assure that the date of the taking of the specimen and the tests results are recorded on the infant's hospital chart and reported to the attending physician. 16-2.18(6)-S1820(9)(10)(d)

e. **treatment** The department may determine the procedure for advising the physicians, parents or legal guardian of the availability of assistance or services. § 50-19-204(2)

f. **follow-up** No mention.

g. **education** No mention.

h. **counseling** The department may determine the procedure for advising the physician, parents, or legal guardian of the availability of counseling. § 50-19-204(2)

i. **research** No mention.

j. **other** The department and the staff of the Boulder River School and hospital shall cooperate to achieve the legislative intent of this part. § 50-19-204 (1)

2. **Are there confidentiality requirements?** No mention.

3. **Is a registry established?** No mention.

C. **For the costs of the program?** No mention.

V. **Are there sanctions to punish non-compliance?** No mention.

NEBRASKA

I. **Is there a statute addressing neonatal genetic screening?** Neb. Rev. Stat. §§ 71-604.01 to -604.04 (1981). See also the statutes regarding birth defects more generally: § 71-645 et seq. (1981).

A. **Does it state an objective?** The screening law states no purpose. A separate act states that in order to provide for the protection and promotion of health of the citizens of the state, the Department of Health shall research causes, prevention, treatment, and cure of birth defects. § 71-645

B. **Does it compel screening?** Mandatory. § 71-604.01

1. **Are there exceptions?** Parents or guardians who are members of an established church may object on religious grounds. § 71-604.01

2. **Does it provide notice to parents and guardians of the right to object?** No.

II. **What does the program screen for and how readily can other tests be added?** Phenylketonuria and hypothyroidism are specified. § 71-604.03 The Director of Health may require tests for other metabolic diseases as they are perfected. § 71-604.01(3)

III. **Does the statute provide for centralization or quality assurance?** No facility is specified. Under the birth defects act, the department may secure necessary scientific, educational, training, technical, administrative, or operational personnel and services including laboratories by contract or otherwise from public or private entities. § 71-647(5)

IV. **Who is responsible . . .**

A. **For each individual screen?** No responsible party is specified; however, responsibility for following the development of the child is primarily the parents' or guardians' and secondarily, the Department of Health's. § 71-604.01(2)

B. **For the program?** The Department of Health, which may promulgate and enforce rules. § 71.604.01

1. **Does the program provide for . . .**

a. **testing** The Department of Health shall prescribe screening procedures (§ 71-604.03) and determine which tests are required (§ 71-604.01(3)).

b. **confirming positive result** The department must prescribe procedures to determine if the syndrome is actually present. § 71-604.01(1)

c. **reporting** Results of these tests may be included in the monthly report to the department on births provided the report is forwarded no later than the 10th day of the month after the test is administered. § 71-604.04

d. **recording** The Director of Health may require that test results be recorded on the birth certificate. § 71-604.01(3)

e. **treatment** No mention.

f. **follow-up** Responsibility for following the development of the child and assuring that those caring for the child are informed of proper treatments is primarily the parents' and secondarily the Department of Health's. § 71-604.01(2)

g. **education** Under the birth defects act, the department may carry on professional education programs for medical students, physicians, nurses, scientists, and technicians in the causes, methods of prevention, treatment, and cure of birth defects. § 71-647(3) The department also may publish annually and distribute to physicians the results of research it undertakes. § 71-647(2)

h. **counseling** Under the birth defects act, the department may conduct and support clinical counseling services in medical facilities. § 71-647(4)

i. **research** Under the birth defects act, the department is empowered to conduct scientific investigations and surveys of the causes of mortality, methods of prevention, treatment and cure of birth defects. § 71-647(1)

2. **Are there confidentiality requirements?** Under the birth defects act, reports of birth defects and allied diseases made by physicians to the department of health are required unless an objection is made by parents on religious grounds. § 71-648 (1) These reports shall remain confidential and not admissible as evidence in any legal action. § 71-648 (2)

3. **Is a registry established?** Under the birth defects act, the Director of Health shall establish a birth defects registry "for the purposes of initiating and conducting investigations of the causes, mortality, methods of prevention, treatment, and cure of birth defects and allied diseases." § 71-646

   a. **Is it mandatory?** Religious exemptions are allowed. § 71-648(1)

   b. **Is it confidential?** Reports and information shall be kept confidential and are inadmissible as evidence in legal proceedings. § 71-648(2) The department may publish analyses that assure that the identities of the individuals concerned cannot be ascertained. § 71-648(2)

C. **For the costs of the program?** No mention.

V. **Are there sanctions to punish non-compliance?** No.

NEVADA

I. **Is there a statute addressing neonatal genetic screening?** Nev. Rev. Stat. § 442.115 (1979).

A. **Does it state an objective?** To discover preventable inheritable disorders leading to mental retardation. § 442.115(1)

B. **Does it compel screening?** Mandatory. § 442.115(2)

1. **Are there exceptions?** Either parent may file a written objection with the person or institution responsible for the exam. § 442.115(4)

2. **Does it provide notice to parents and guardians of the right to object?** No mention. A form letter to the parents from the Bureau of Children's Services states that the law "requires" testing, giving no indication of any grounds for exceptions.

II. **What does the program screen for and how readily can other tests be added?** Preventable inheritable disorders leading to mental retardation specified by the state board of health, upon recommendation of the state health officer. § 442.115 (1)

III. **Does the statute provide for centralization or quality assurance?** No mention.

IV. **Who is responsible . . .**

A. **For each individual screen?** Any physician, midwife, nurse, maternity home or hospital attending or assisting the infant or the mother at childbirth. § 442.115(2)

B. **For the program?** The state board of health in consultation with the state health officer. § 442.115(1)

1. **Does the program provide for . . .**

a. **testing** The state Board of Health shall adopt regulations governing examinations and tests. § 442.115(1)

b. **confirming positive result** No mention.

c. **reporting** The party responsible for testing shall report a positive result to the local health officer. § 442.115(3)(a)

d. **recording** No mention.

e. **treatment** If the test is positive, the party responsible for testing will discuss the condition with the parents and inform them about the necessary treatment. § 442.115(3)(b)

f. **follow-up** No mention.

g. **education** No mention.

h. **counseling** No mention.

i. **research** No mention.

2. **Are there confidentiality requirements?** No mention.

3. **Is a registry established?** No mention.

C. **For the costs of the program?** No mention.

V. **Are there sanctions to punish non-compliance?** No mention.

NEW HAMPSHIRE

I. **Is there a statute addressing neonatal genetic screening?** N.H. Rev. Stat. Ann. § 132:10-a,b,c (1978). The Department of Health and Welfare Division of Public Health Services Bureau for the Handicapped Children has published "Recommendations for Newborn Screening Specimen Collection" (March 18, 1983).

A. **Does it state an objective?** No mention.

B. **Does it compel screening?** Mandatory. § 132:10-a

1. **Are there exceptions?** Parental objection. § 132:10-c

2. **Does it provide notice to parents and guardians of the right to object?** No mention.

II. **What does the program screen for and how readily can other tests be added?** Phenylketonuria. § 132:10-a A letter to physicians introducing the recommendations states that, as of July 1, 1983, testing for phenylketonuria, galactosomia, homocystinuria, maple syrup urine disease and hypothyroidism shall be performed by the New England Regional Program for testing.

III. **Does the statute provide for centralization or quality assurance?** No mention in the statute. The recommendations indicate that testing shall be accomplished through the New England Regional Program.

IV. **Who is responsible . . .**

A. **For each individual screen?** The physician and/or hospital attending a newborn. § 132:10-a The recommendations indicate that if there is no physician, the family should be advised to contact their local public health nurse.

B. **For the program?** The Director of the Division of Public Health Services shall make rules and regulations. § 132:10-b

1. **Does the program provide for . . .**

a. **testing** The director of the division of public health services shall make rules and regulations pertaining to such tests as accepted medical practice indicates. § 132:10-b The recommendations outline the procedure for blood sample collection pertaining to: full term newborns (1A), premature infants (1B), exchange transfusion infants (1C), sick infants (1D), transferred babies (1E), infants born outside of a hospital (1F). Normally a blood specimen should be collected at the time of discharge but not before 48 hours of life. 1A The recommendations indicate that rescreening is recommended only if the infant is discharged prior to 48 hours of life or has been tranfused before a first blood specimen could be collected.

b. confirming positive result No mention.

c. reporting No mention in the statute. According to the Recommendations, the test results shall be sent to the hospital, which makes a copy of it and places the copy in the physician's box. Positive screening results shall be called to the physician.

d. recording No mention in the statute. The recommendations state that test results shall be recorded on report forms one of which is returned to the hospital.

e. treatment No mention.

f. follow-up No mention.

g. education No mention.

h. counseling No mention.

i. research No mention.

2. Are there confidentiality requirements? No mention.

3. Is a registry established? No mention.

C. For the costs of the program? No mention.

V. Are there sanctions to punish non-compliance? No mention.

NEW JERSEY

I. **Is there a statute addressing neonatal genetic screening?** N.J. Stat. Ann. § 26:2-110 et seq. (West Supp. 1982-83). See also Hereditary Disorders Act § 26:5B-1 et seq. (West Supp. 1982-83).

A. **Does it state an objective?** To detect preventable biochemical disorders which may cause mental retardation or other permanent disabilities. § 26:2-110

B. **Does it compel screening?** Mandatory. § 26:2-111

1. **Are there exceptions?** Parents may object on religious grounds. § 26:2-111

2. **Does it provide notice to parents and guardians of the right to object?** No mention.

II. **What does the program screen for and how readily can other tests be added?** Phenylketonuria, hypothyroidism, galactosemia, and other preventable biochemical disorders which may cause mental retardation or other permanent disabilities (§ 26:2-110), if reliable and efficient testing for these other disorders is available (§ 26:2-111).

III. **Does the statute provide for centralization or quality assurance?** No mention.

IV. **Who is responsible . . .**

A. **For each individual screen?** No mention.

B. **For the program?** The Commissioner of Health, who shall issue regulations. § 26:2-111

1. **Does the program provide for . . .**

a. **testing** The commissioner shall approve the manner and the types of tests required. § 26:2-111

b. **confirming positive result** No mention.

c. **reporting** No mention.

d. **recording** No mention.

e. **treatment** Under the hereditary disorders act, the Department of Health shall establish guidelines for the education, treatment and referral for medical treatment and financial assistance of affected persons. § 26:5B-4b

f. **follow-up** The commissioner shall provide a program of reviewing and follow-up on positive cases. § 26:2-111

g. **education** The Department shall conduct an intensive educational and training program among physicians, hospitals, public health nurses and the public concerning the nature and tests for the detection of biochemical disorders covered by the act. § 26:2-111 See also § 26:5B-4d

h. **counseling** No mention.

i. **research** No mention.

j. **other** The Department of Health shall consult with the Commissioner of Insurance in identifying arbitrary and unreasonable discrimination against people with hereditary disorders and their families in insurance coverage. § 26:5B-4(e)

2. **Are there confidentiality requirements?** The information compiled on newborn infants and their families shall be confidential and not divulged or made public so as to disclose the identity of any person, except as provided by law. § 26:2-111

   a. **Who has access?** Information may be used by the department and agencies to carry out this act. § 26:2-111

3. **Is a registry established?** Under a separate statute, the Department is required to establish and maintain a birth defects registry "which shall contain a confidential record of all birth defects that occur in New Jersey and any other information that the department deems necessary and appropriate in order to conduct thorough and complete epidemiologic surveys of birth defects." N.J. Stat. Ann. § 26:8-40.21 (West Supp. 1984-85)

C. **For the costs of the program?** The department may charge a reasonable fee for tests performed. The amount and collection procedures shall be determined by the commissioner. § 26:2-111

V. **Are there sanctions to punish non-compliance?** No mention.

NEW MEXICO

I. Is there a statute addressing neonatal genetic screening? N.M. Stat. Ann. § 24-1-6 (Supp. 1982). The Health and Environment Department has promulgated "Newborn Screening Program Regulations" § 100 et seq. (July 1, 1979).

A. Does it state an objective? No mention.

B. Does it compel screening? Mandatory. § 24-1-6(A)

1. Are there exceptions? Parents may object in writing. § 24-1-6 (A), (D)

2. Does it provide notice to parents and guardians of the right to object? After being informed of the reasons for the test, the parents may object. § 24-1-6(A) See also § 301 of the regulations.

II. What does the program screen for and how readily can other tests be added? Phenylketonuria and other congenital diseases that the secretary of health and environment specifies on the recommendations of the New Mexico Pediatrics Society. § 24-1-6(A) Under the regulations, the other diseases for which screening is required are hypothyroidism, galactosemia, homocystinuria, maple syrup urine disease, and sickle cell anemia. § 103(B)

III. Does the statute provide for centralization or quality assurance? The department may institute laboratory services or may contract with another agency or state to provide testing. § 24-1-6(B) The regulations specify that testing shall be done through "a regional screening program established at the Colorado Department of Health or, if the Department shall hereafter so require, at the Scientific Laboratory Division or at a laboratory approved for purposes of such testing by the Scientific Laboratory Division." § 102

IV. Who is responsible . . .

A. For each individual screen? Hospitals or institutions with childbirth facilities. § 24-1-6(D) Under the regulations, if a child is not born in a hospital, the attending physician, nurse, nurse-midwife, midwife or responsible person shall arrange for specimen collection. § 203

B. For the program?

1. Does the program provide for . . .

a. testing No mention in the statute. The regulations provide extensive guidelines for the timing of testing (§ 200 et seq.), require that the specimen be sent for testing within 24 hours of its collection (§ 204), and provide for collection of a second phenylketonuria sample before the child is two weeks old (§ 206).

b. confirming positive result No mention.

c. reporting No mention in the statute. The regulations require immediate reporting of positive or questionable results to the department's Child Development Center and the physician and provide that "[c]ontact with the parents of the child will be reported to the hospital and physician for placement in the child's record." § 207

d. recording No mention.

e. treatment No mention.

f. follow-up No mention.

g. education The Department shall carry on an educational program among physicians, hospitals, public health nurses and the public. § 24-1-6(C)

h. counseling No mention.

i. research No mention.

2. Are there confidentiality requirements? No mention.

3. Is a registry established? No mention.

C. For the costs of the program? No mention.

V. Are there sanctions to punish non-compliance? No mention.

NEW YORK

I. **Is there a statute addressing neonatal genetic screening?** N.Y. Pub. Health Law § 2500 et seq. (McKinney 1972) and N.Y. Pub. Health Law § 2730 et seq. (McKinney 1972). Regulations are set forth in N.Y. Admin. Code tit. 10, § 69.1 et seq. (1978).

A. **Does it state an objective?** To prevent mortality, diseases and defects of childhood and promote child health. § 2500(1)

B. **Does it compel screening?** Mandatory. § 2500-a(a)

1. **Are there exceptions?** A parent who belongs to recognized religious organization whose teachings and tenets are contrary to testing may object on religious grounds as long as the responsible party is notified. § 2500-a(b); § 69.4 (regulations).

2. **Does it provide notice to parents and guardians of the right to object?** No mention.

II. **What does the program screen for and how readily can other tests be added?** Phenylketonuria, homozygous sickle cell disease, hypothyroidism, branched-chain ketonuria, galactosemia, homocystinuria, adenosine deaminase deficiency, histindinemia, and such other diseases and conditions as the commissioner may designate. § 2500-a(a).

III. **Does the statute provide for centralization or quality assurance?** No mention in the statute. The regulations specify that testing should be performed by a laboratory designated for such purpose by the State Commissioner of Health. § 69.1

IV. **Who is responsible . . .**

A. **For each individual screen?** The administrative officer or other person in charge of each institution caring for infants twenty-eight days old or younger and the person required to register the birth of a child. § 2500-a(a) Under the regulations, the latter has responsibility if the infant is born outside of an institution and has not subsequently been admitted to an institution for newborn care. § 69.2(d)

B. **For the program?** The Commissioner of the Department of Health. § 2500

1. **Does the program provide for . . .**

a. **testing** Testing for diseases designated by the commissioner shall be performed at such times and in such manner as prescribed by the commissioner. § 2500-a(a) The regulations include provisions for the test procedure (§ 69.1) and the time and place for testing (§ 69.2). Infants shall be tested on the day of discharge but not later than the 14th day of life unless this is medically contraindicated. (§ 69.2, (a), (c))

b. **confirming positive result** No mention.

c. **reporting** Birth defects and genetic diseases shall be reported by physicians, hospitals, and persons in attendance at births in the manner and on such forms as prescribed by the commissioner. § 2733.1

d. **recording** Recording shall be performed at such times and in such manner as prescribed by the Commissioner. § 2500-a(a) The regulations specify that it is the task of the administrator of the responsible institution and the person required to register the birth of the child to have the test results recorded on the infant's chart. § 69.3(d)

e. **treatment** No mention.

f. **follow-up** No mention.

g. **education** The commissioner shall carry on professional education programs for medical students, physicians, nurses, scientists and technicians. § 2732(c)

h. **counseling** The commissioner shall conduct and support counseling services. § 2732(d)

i. **research** The commissioner shall conduct scientific investigations and surveys of the causes, mortality, methods of treatment, prevention and cure of birth defects and genetic and allied diseases. § 2732(a) To that end, the commissioner shall establish a birth defects institute. § 2731

j. **other** The commissioner shall periodically publish the results of investigations and collate the publications to distribute them to qualified scientists and physicians. § 2732(b).

2. **Are there confidentiality requirements?** No mention specifically covering newborn screening.

3. **Is a registry established?** Birth defects and genetic and allied diseases shall be reported by physicians, hospitals and birth attendants. § 2733(1)

a. **Is it mandatory?** Yes. § 2733

b. **Is it confidential?**Reports and information shall be kept confidential and shall not be admissible as evidence in an action or proceeding in any court. § 2733(2) But the commissioner may publish analyses without identifying individuals. § 2733(2)

C. **For the costs of the program?** No mention.

V. **Are there sanctions to punish non-compliance?** No mention.

NORTH CAROLINA

I. **Is there a statute addressing neonatal genetic screening?** N.C. Gen. Stat. § 143B-194 (1983). The Division of Health Services of the Department of Human Resources has established a "PKU and Hypothyroid Protocol."

A. **Does it state an objective?** No mention.

B. **Does it compel screening?** Testing is voluntary. § 143B-194 Testing for sickle cell syndrome and related disorders shall be available to any person requesting it. § 143B-195

II. **What does the program screen for and how readily can other tests be added?** The statute authorizes the Secretary of Human Resources to initiate pilot programs for voluntary testing for sickle cell syndrome and related genetic disorders. § 143B-195 The protocol covers screening for phenylketonuria and hypothyroidism.

III. **Does the statute provide for centralization or quality assurance?** No mention.

IV. **Who is responsible . . .**

A. **For each individual screen?** No mention.

B. **For the program?** The Secretary of Human Resources. § 143B-195

1. **Does the program provide for . . .**

a. **testing** Yes, on a pilot basis. § 143B-195 The Protocol provides extensive guidelines on laboratory analysis of samples. The Protocol requires that the maximum turnaround time from receipt of the specimen to notification of the physician shall not exceed two weeks. II (I)

b. **confirming positive result** No mention in the statute. The Protocol provides extensive guidelines for the follow-up of abnormal test results using repeat analyses. I (E)

c. **reporting** No mention in the statute. According to the Protocol, the reporting procedure to be followed for phenylketonuria testing depends on the phenylalanine level. I If the levels are in a range that is considered to indicate a high risk, the laboratory immediately notifies the physician or health department by certified mail and sends a copy to the medical records office of the appropriate hospital. I (D) (2) The program manager notifies the primary physician or health department by phone within one day of the analysis. I(D)(3) Similar reporting procedures exist with respect to hypothyroidism testing. II, II (E)

d. **recording** No mention.

e. **treatment** No mention.

f. **follow-up** No mention.

g. **education** Yes, on a pilot basis. § 143B-196 No program for voluntary testing shall begin earlier than 60 days after an adequate and effective educational program. § 143B-196

h. **counseling** Yes, on a pilot basis. § 143B-195 Counseling shall be done only by adequately trained and certified persons. § 143B-196

i. **research** No mention.

2. **Are there confidentiality requirements?** No mention.

3. **Is a registry established?** No mention.

C. **For the costs of the program?** Testing and counseling for sickle cell syndrome and related genetic disorders shall be furnished without cost to persons requesting it. § 143B-195

V. **Are there sanctions to punish non-compliance?** No mention.

NORTH DAKOTA

I. **Is there a statute addressing neonatal genetic screening?** N.D. Cent. Code § 25-17-01 et seq. (1978). The North Dakota State Department of Health Division of Maternal and Child Health has issued a "Newborn Metabolic Screening Policy Statement" (November 1982).

A. **Does it state an objective?** To provide screening, diagnostic, and treatment control tests on a statewide basis. § 25-17-01(2)

B. **Does it compel screening?** Mandatory. § 25-17-04.

1. **Are there exceptions?** Parents may object on religious grounds. § 25-17-04.

2. **Does it provide notice to parents and guardians of the right to object?** The Policy Statement provides that "[b]rief discussion of newborn metabolic testing by physicians and nurses with the parents is recommended."

II. **What does the program screen for and how readily can other tests be added?** Phenylketonuria and other errors of metabolism. § 25-17-01(1) The Policy Statement specifically mentions phenylketonuria and hypothyroidism.

III. **Does the statute provide for centralization or quality assurance?** No specific mention. The policy statement requires that specimens be sent to the State Public Health Laboratory.

IV. **Who is responsible . . .**

A. **For each individual screen?** The physician attending a newborn. § 25-17-04

B. **For the program?** The state Department of Health shall establish standards and methods of testing. § 25-17-02

1. **Does the program provide for . . .**

a. **testing** The department shall establish standards and methods of testing. § 25-17-02

b. **confirming positive result** The State Department of Public Health shall follow up positive tests with the physician to determine the exact diagnosis. § 25-17-03(1) The policy statement specifies that the Division will provide "payment for serum phenylalanine and tyrosine analysis necessary for confirmation of the diagnosis."

c. **reporting** The physician attending a case must report the case to the State Department of Public Health, unless the parents object on religious grounds. § 25-17-04 The Policy Statement provides that positive results be reported by phone to the physician by the Division of Maternal and Child Health and that a follow-up report letter be sent both to the physician and to the parents.

d. **recording** No mention.

e. **treatment** The department shall make arrangements for treatment where indicated and the family is unable to pay. § 25-17-03(2)

f. **follow-up** The department shall follow up positive cases with the attending physician to determine the exact diagnosis. § 25-17-03(1) The policy statement provides for various follow-up services including assistance with dietary management, in-home follow-up, and special formulae free of charge to the needy.

g. **education** The department shall undertake an intensive educational program among physicians, hospitals, public health nurses, and the public. § 25-17-01(1)

h. **counseling** No mention.

i. **research** No mention.

j. **other** The Policy Statement provides that the Division of Maternal and Child Health will provide "[i]nformation and counseling regarding the issue of maternal PKU for young women with PKU who are anticipating child-bearing."

2. **Are there confidentiality requirements?** No mention.

3. **Is a registry established?** The State Department of Public Health shall maintain a registry. § 25-17-03(3)

a. **Is it mandatory?** No mention.

b. **Is it confidential?** No mention.

C. **For the costs of the program?** The department will make arrangements for treatment where the family is unable to pay the costs. § 25-17-03(2) The policy statement specifies that the Division will provide "payment for serum phenylalanine and tyrosine analysis necessary for confirmation of the diagnosis."

V. **Are there sanctions to punish non-compliance?** No mention.

OHIO

I. Is there a statute addressing neonatal genetic screening? Ohio Rev. Code Ann. § 3701.501, 502 (Baldwin 1984). The Public Health Council has promulgated regulations which are set forth in Ohio Admin. Code § 3701-45-01 (1981) and § 3701-49-01 (1983).

A. Does it state an objective? No mention.

B. Does it compel screening? Mandatory. § 3701.501(A)

1. Are there exceptions? Parents may object on religious grounds. § 3701.501(B)

2. Does it provide notice to parents and guardians of the right to object? Rules adopted by the public health council shall prescribe a method for giving notice of the proposed tests to the newborn's parents. § 3701.501(A) The regulations provide that each hospital shall give parents printed information on the program. § 3701-45-01(C)(1) In an out-of-the-hospital birth, the attending physician or midwife provides the material (§ 3701-45-01(C)(2)) or if neither are present, the health commissioner of the health district in which the birth occurred provides the material (§ 3701-45-01(C)(3)).

II. What does the program screen for and how readily can other tests be added? Requires testing for phenylketonuria, homocystinuria, galactosemia, and hypothyroidism. Other tests may be required if the disorders cause disability if undiagnosed and untreated and are treatable and no additional samples are required. § 3701.501(A)(1) and (2)

III. Does the statute provide for centralization or quality assurance? All tests shall be performed by the authorized laboratory. § 3701.501(A)

IV. Who is responsible . . .

A. For each individual screen? The person required to file a certificate of birth. § 3701.501(A)

B. For the program? The Public Health Council, which may adopt rules and regulations. § 3701.501(A)

1. Does the program provide for . . .

a. testing The Public Health Council determines what diseases shall be tested for and laboratory methods and procedures. § 3701.501(A) The regulations provide extensive guidelines for testing, including that the specimens be sent to the laboratory no later than 48 hours after collection (§ 3701-45-01(D)(4)), and that the tests be completed within three working days of submission (§ 3701-45-01(B)(1)).

b. **confirming positive result** No mention in the statute. The regulations require that any abnormal or suspicious test result be followed by a second specimen submitted by the person who submitted the first. § 3701-45-01(B)(2)

c. **reporting** No mention in the statute. The regulations require that test results be promptly transmitted to the person who submitted the specimen or to the hospital in the manner prescribed and provided by the director of health. § 3701-45-01 (B)(1)

d. **recording** No mention in the statute. The regulations provide that records on each infant tested be kept for not less than 21 years. § 3701-45-01(B)(3)

e. **treatment** The director of health shall assist in developing treatment programs and provide for habilitation. § 3701.502(A)

f. **follow-up** No mention.

g. **education** The director of health assists in developing programs of education. § 3701.502(A)

h. **counseling** The director of health assists in developing counseling programs. § 3701.502(A)

i. **research** No mention.

2. **Are there confidentiality requirements?** No mention.

3. **Is a registry established?** No mention.

C. **For the costs of the program?** The regulations set a fee of six dollars for each sample tested. § 3701-49-01(A) That charge is waived if parents are unable to pay, if rescreening is necessary, or if the tests are submitted by a local health department for a newborn delivered at home. § 3701-49-01(B)(10)

V. **Are there sanctions to punish non-compliance?** No mention.

OKLAHOMA

I. Is there a statute addressing neonatal genetic screening? Okla. Stat. Ann. tit. 63 §§ 1-553, 1-554 (West Supp. 1982-83). The Board of Health has adopted regulations as of June 13, 1971, "Rules and Regulations Specifying Approved Tests and Requirements for Approved Laboratories Performing Tests for Phenylketonuria," and has supplemented these with memoranda to hospital administrators.

- **A. Does it state an objective?** To prevent mental retardation resulting from inborn metabolic disorders. § 1-533
- **B. Does it compel screening?** The Board of Health may make testing mandatory if the public is negligent in accepting testing and the board considers it in the public interest to do so. § 1-534
  1. **Are there exceptions?** Parents may object on religious grounds. § 1-534
  2. **Does it provide notice to parents and guardians of the right to object?** No mention.

II. What does the program screen for and how readily can other tests be added? The statute provides for testing for phenylketonuria and related inborn metabolic disorders. § 1-533 According to a communication from the Oklahoma State Department of Health, hypothyroidism testing was introduced in 1980.

III. Does the statute provide for centralization or quality assurance? The Board of Health may set up laboratory facilities, use existing facilities, or approve other laboratories. § 1-534. The regulations require that testing for phenylketonuria be carried out in the Oklahoma State Department of Health Laboratory or in a laboratory approved by the commissioner.

IV. Who is responsible . . .

- **A. For each individual screen?** No mention.
- **B. For the program?** The Board of Health, which shall make such rules and regulations as accepted medical practice indicates § 1-534.
  1. **Does the program provide for . . .**
     - **a. testing** The board is empowered to make rules and regulations pertaining to tests. § 1-534. The regulations that have been adopted specify the acceptable methods of screening. In a memorandum to hospital administrators concerning expansion of testing to include screening for

hypothyroidism, the board promulgates guidelines for the timing of phenylketonuria and hypothyroidism testing.

b. **confirming positive result** No mention. A letter from the Department of Health to public health nurses specifies a procedure for repeat tests.

c. **reporting** No mention in the statute. The regulations provide that the laboratory director immediately report positive results to the department.

d. **recording** No mention.

e. **treatment** No mention.

f. **follow-up** No mention. According to a memorandum from the Department of Health, public health nurses are to see that abnormal results have been followed by a second test and that the patient and family are receiving follow-up care.

g. **education** The board shall undertake an educational program among physicians, hospitals, public health nurses, and the public. § 1-533

h. **counseling** No mention.

i. **research** No mention.

2. **Are there confidentiality requirements?** No mention.

3. **Is a registry established?** No mention in the statute.

C. **For the costs of the program?** The board may charge a reasonable fee as long as no child is denied laboratory tests because of the parents' inability to pay. § 1-534

V. **Are there sanctions to punish non-compliance?** No mention.

OREGON

I. **Is there a statute addressing neonatal genetic screening?** Or. Rev. Stat. § 433.285 et seq. (1981). Regulations are set forth in Or. Admin. R. 333-24-210 (1983).

A. **Does it state an objective?** The prevention of mental retardation. § 433.285(1)

B. **Does it compel screening?** Mandatory. § 433.285(1)

1. **Are there exceptions?** Parents may object if they sign a statement that the infant is being reared as an adherent to a religion opposed to testing. § 433.285(3) In the event of a religious exemption, the person otherwise responsible for submitting a specimen must submit a completed statement to the state laboratory signed by the infant's parents. The regulations provide a sample of the statement. R. 333-24-235(1)(a)

2. **Does it provide notice to parents and guardians of the right to object?** No mention.

II. **What does the program screen for and how readily can other tests be added?** Phenylketonuria and other metabolic diseases. § 433.285(1) The regulations require testing for phenylketonuria, maple syrup urine disease, hypermethioninemia, tyrosinemia, galactosemia, and hypothyroidism. R. 333-24-210(1)(a)

III. **Does the statute provide for centralization or quality assurance?** No mention in the statute. The regulations require that all specimens that are submitted to the state laboratory for testing use kits provided by the state laboratory. R. 333-24-220(1) The regulations also specify the methods of testing and provide that no other method shall be approved unless it meets or exceeds these methods in respect to specificity, sensitivity, and precision of the assay. R. 333-24-230

IV. **Who is responsible . . .**

A. **For each individual screen?** The Health Division shall by rule specify the persons responsible for submitting specimens. § 433.285(2) According to the regulations, the responsibility of assuring that specimens are submitted lies first with the hospital or health care facility, secondly with the physician and if no physician is in attendance, it is the responsibility of the parent or legal guardian. R. 333-24-215(1)(a)

B. **For the program?** The Health Division. §§ 433.285, 433.290

1. **Does the program provide for . . .**

a. **testing** The Health Division shall approve tests (433.285(1)), specify the diseases for testing (§ 433.285(2)), and specify the time and manner of testing (§ 433.285(2)). The regulations specify guidelines for the manner of submitting specimens (R. 333-24-220), the time of collecting specimens (R. 333-24-215(1)(b) and -225), and methods of testing (R. 333-24-230). Generally, specimens should be collected within 10 days after birth (R. 333-24-225) and sent to the laboratory within 24 hours of collection (R. 333-24-220(2)). The regulations generally prohibit the use of urine specimens to detect metabolic diseases, since the tests are unreliable (R. 333-24-2); however, if the religious exception has been involved, urine testing of the infant is required (R. 333-24-235(2)(a)).

b. **confirming positive result** No mention.

c. **reporting** All physicians, public health nurses and hospital administrators shall report the discovery of cases to the Health Division. § 433.295(1) The Health Division furnishes reporting forms. § 433.295(2)

d. **recording** No mention.

e. **treatment** No mention.

f. **follow-up** No mention.

g. **education** The Health Division shall institute an intensive educational program for physicians, hospitals, public health nurses and the public. § 433.290

h. **counseling** No mention.

i. **research** No mention.

j. **other** Another statute, Ore. Rev. Stat § 352.058(1) (1981) provides that it is state policy to encourage amniocentesis. The statute provides for the establishment of an amniocentesis program at the Oregon Health Sciences University (§ 352.058(2)) and sets forth criteria for eligibility (§ 352.058(3)). It also provides that the university establish a graduated fee schedule, develop an educational program for physicians and the public, assure that genetic counseling is given in conjunction with the amniocentesis, and provide that participation shall be voluntary. § 352.058(4)

2. **Are there confidentiality requirements?** No mention.

3. **Is a registry established?** No mention.

C. **For the costs of the program?** The Health Division shall establish the manner of payment of fees (§ 433.285(2)), provided that no infant be refused because of parents' inability to pay the fee. (§ 433.285(4)) The regulations require that the person responsible for submitting the specimen pay a fee of $4.40 per specimen (R. 333-24-240(1)(a)) but that a practitioner or patient may claim an exemption from this fee by submitting a written statement asserting inability to pay (R. 333-24-240(5)(a)).

V. Are there sanctions to punish non-compliance? No mention.

PENNSYLVANIA

I. Is there a statute addressing neonatal genetic screening? Pa. Stat. Ann. tit. 35 § 621 (Purdon 1977). The regulations are set forth in 28 Pa. Admin. Code, § 28.1 et seq. (1980).

A. Does it state an objective? No mention.

B. Does it compel screening? Mandatory. § 621

1. Are there exceptions? Parents may object on religious grounds. § 621 (The regulations contain a similar provision, § 28.3(b).)

2. Does it provide notice to parents and guardians of the right to object? No mention in the statute. The regulations provide that the health care facility or practitioner responsible for care of the pregnant woman or mother shall provide her with an explanatory screening pamphlet supplied by the department. § 28.11

II. What does the program screen for and how readily can other tests be added? Phenylketonuria and other metabolic disease specified by the Advisory Health Board. § 621 The regulations provide for testing for phenylketonuria and hypothyroidism. § 28.2

III. Does the statute provide for centralization or quality assurance? No mention in the statute. The regulations require that specimens be sent to laboratories specified by the Department. § 28.4

IV. Who is responsible . . .

A. For each individual screen? A hospital or institution or physician caring for newborns. § 621; § 28.21 (regulations)

B. For the program? The Advisory Health Board of the State Department of Health. § 621

1. Does the program provide for . . .

a. testing The Advisory Health Board of the State Department of Health approves tests. § 621 The regulations specify what those approved tests are (§ 28.3), and how specimens should be collected and tested (§§ 28.4, 28.21 et seq.). They provide that specimens must be submitted within 48 hours of collection. § 28.4

b. confirming positive result The regulations provide that if the results of a test are presumptive positive, a confirmatory specimen is required. §§ 28.29, 28.30(a)(1), 28.31(a)

c. reporting No mention in the statute. According to the regulations, negative results must be reported within seven days after the laboratory obtains the results. § 28.24(a) The health care facility or practitioner that receives presumptive positive results "shall promptly notify the parents or guardian and arrange for follow-up and shall enter the report of the result into the patient's medical record." § 28.27 The department must be notified if the parents cannot be located within 48 hours. § 28.27

d. recording No mention in the statute. According to the regulations, the negative results shall be recorded in the patient's medical records. § 28.24(b) The Department's summary of the responsibilities of health care facilities and physicians similarly requires that all test results, including those of the follow-up program, be recorded in the patient's medical record.

e. treatment No mention.

f. follow-up Under the regulations, if the phenylketonuria confirmatory test is positive, the department will arrange for referral, diagnosis, treatment, habilitative and other followup services. § 28.30(b) If confirmatory tests for hypothyroidism are positive, the department will provide consultative services. § 28.31(b)

g. education No mention.

h. counseling No mention.

i. research No mention.

j. other According to the regulations, if a child exhibits signs suggestive of metabolic disease and has not already been determined to be affected, the health care facility or practitioner shall collect a blood specimen for metabolic disease testing. § 28.28

2. Are there confidentiality requirements? No mention.

3. Is a registry established? No mention.

C. For the costs of the program? No mention.

V. Are there sanctions to punish non-compliance? No mention.

RHODE ISLAND

I. Is there a statute addressing neonatal genetic screening? R.I. Gen. Laws § 23-13-12 (1976). The Rhode Island Department of Health has established rules for phenylketonuria testing (September 8, 1964) and has implemented a collection schedule for specimens for screening for hypothyroidism, phenylketonuria, galactosemia, maple syrup urine disease, and homocystinuria, entitled "Newborn Screening Program Specimen Collection Schedule".

A. Does it state an objective? No mention.

B. Does it compel screening? Mandatory. § 23-13-12.

1. **Are there exceptions?** Parents may object on religious grounds. § 23-13-12; 3 (rules)
2. **Does it provide notice to parents and guardians of the right to object?** No mention.

II. What does the program screen for and how readily can other tests be added? Phenylketonuria. § 23-13-12 The "Newborn Screening Program Specimen Collection Schedule" indicates that the newborn screening program includes testing for hypothyroidism, phenylketonuria, galactosemia, maple syrup urine disease, and homocystinuria.

III. Does the statute provide for centralization or quality assurance? No mention in the statute. The rules require that specimens for phenylketonuria testing be sent to the Department laboratory or to a facility where testing has been approved by the Department. 3

IV. Who is responsible . . .

A. For each individual screen? The physician attending the newborn. § 23-13-12

B. For the program? The Department of Health, which shall promulgate rules. § 23-13-12

1. **Does the program provide for . . .**

   a. **testing** The Department of Health shall make such rules pertaining to such tests as accepted medical practice indicates. § 23-13-12 The "Collection Schedule" specifies the manner and timing of collecting and submitting specimens for:

   1) full term newborns

2) premature infants

3) exchange transfused babies

4) sick babies

5) transferred babies

In the case of full term infants a specimen should be obtained at the time of discharge or on or before the fourth day after birth. If discharged before 48 hours a second specimen may be requested.

b. **confirming positive result** No mention.

c. **reporting** No mention.

d. **recording** No mention.

e. **treatment** No mention.

f. **follow-up** No mention.

g. **education** No mention.

h. **counseling** No mention.

i. **research** No mention.

2. **Are there confidentiality requirements?** No mention.

3. **Is a registry established?** No mention.

C. **For the costs of the program?** No mention. The rules state that the Department will provide necessary materials and laboratory analysis for phenylketonuria testing on request, at no charge. 2

V. **Are there sanctions to punish non-compliance?** No mention.

SOUTH CAROLINA

I. **Is there a statute addressing neonatal genetic screening?** S.C. Ann. Code § 44-37-30 (Law & Coop. Supp. 1983). The Department of Health and Environmental Control promulgated Metabolic Disorders Screening Program Rules and Regulations and Official Departmental Instructions (1980).

A. **Does it state an objective?** No mention.

B. **Does it compel screening?** Mandatory. § 44-37-30.

1. **Are there exceptions?** Parents may object on religious grounds. § 44-37-30

2. **Does it provide notice to parents and guardians of the right to object?** No mention in the statute. The Official Department Instructions provide that prior to sample collection, the parents shall be given information concerning the screening and the name of the physician from whom they can receive the results. They also state that the "provision of the screening test is covered under the informed consent signed by the parents at the hospital."

II. **What does the program screen for and how readily can other tests be added?** Inborn metabolic errors. § 44-37-30 The regulations specifically require testing for phenylketonuria and hypothyroidism. § B

III. **Does the statute provide for centralization or quality assurance?** No mention in the statute. The regulations require that the Bureau of Laboratories adopt laboratory standards for testing in accordance with official departmental instructions. § C

IV. **Who is responsible . . .**

A. **For each individual screen?** To be determined by the Board of Health and Environmental Control. § 44-37-30 According to the Official Departmental Instructions, the attending physician is responsible for collecting the sample and sending it to the laboratory that same day. If there is no attending physician, the specimen will be collected by authorized personnel in the hospital. If born outside of the hospital without an attending physician, the parents or guardian must notify the County Health Department within three days of delivery. The regulations set out the responsibilities of personnel and parents in screening concerning births both in and outside of a hospital. § D

B. **For the program?** The Board of Health and Environmental Control, which shall prescribe rules and regulations. § 44-37-30

1. **Does the program provide for . . .**

   a. **testing** The Board of Health and Environmental Control shall prescribe the tests to be performed and the procedures for testing. § 44-37-30 The regulations list the type of testing to be performed (§ C) and the manner of collection (§ D).

   b. **confirming positive result** No mention.

   c. **reporting** No mention in the statute. According to the regulations, test results are forwarded by the laboratory to the attending physician, who then informs the parents or guardian. § E.

   d. **recording** The Board of Health and Environmental Control shall prescribe the procedures for recording results. § 44-37-30

   e. **treatment** No mention.

   f. **follow-up** No mention in the statute. According to the regulations, the attending physician "must initiate appropriate medical follow-up and diagnosis on abnormals" or, if that is not possible, must contact appropriate medical resource at the Bureau of Maternal and Child Care. § E(4)

   g. **education** No mention.

   h. **counseling** No mention.

   i. **research** No mention.

   j. **other** According to the regulations, the hospital "must review the patient record for each infant born in the hospital no later than ten (10) days after delivery to ensure that specimen was collected and submitted." § D(2)(e)

2. **Are there confidentiality requirements?** No mention.

3. **Is a registry established?** No mention.

C. **For the costs of the program?** No mention.

V. **Are there sanctions to punish non-compliance?** Any person who fails to comply shall be deemed guilty of misdemeanor and shall be fined not more than $100 or imprisoned not more than 30 days. § 44-37-30

SOUTH DAKOTA

I. **Is there a statute addressing neonatal genetic screening?** S.D. Codified Laws Ann. § 34-24-16 et seq. (1977 and Supp. 1984).

   A. **Does it state an objective?** To prevent mental retardation. § 34-24-16 (Supp. 1984)

   B. **Does it compel screening?** Mandatory. § 34-24-17 (1977)

      1. **Are there exceptions?** Parents may object on religious grounds in writing to the physician in attendance or the person responsible for ordering the test. § 34-24-17 (1977)

      2. **Does it provide notice to parents and guardians of the right to object?** No mention.

II. **What does the program screen for and how readily can other tests be added?** Phenylketonuria, hypothyroidism, and metabolic disorders as prescribed by the Department of Health. § 34-24-18 (Supp. 1984)

III. **Does the statute provide for centralization or quality assurance?** Where facilities are not available, the Department of Health shall perform the test or may contract with any qualified laboratory for testing. § 34-24-19 (Supp. 1984) According to a 1983 communication from the department of health, specimens are evaluated for phenylketonuria and hypothyroidism in five private laboratories throughout the state.

IV. **Who is responsible . . .**

   A. **For each individual screen?** No mention.

   B. **For the program?** The State Department of Health. § 34-24-16 (Supp. 1984)

      1. **Does the program provide for . . .**

         a. **testing** The State Department of Health shall prescribe the method of screening (§ 34-24-17 (1977)), determine which diseases will be screened for (§§ 34-24-18, 34-24-22 (Supp. 1984)), and arrange for testing if the report shows it was not done (§ 34-24-20 (Supp. 1984)).

         b. **confirming positive result** The State Department of Health shall prescribe procedures for determining if the syndrome is actually present when the test shows a presumptive positive. § 34-24-21 (Supp. 1984)

c. **reporting** Results of tests shall be sent to the State Department of Health on report forms furnished to all physicians, hospitals and public health nurses by the department. § 34-24-23 (1977)

d. **recording** No mention.

e. **treatment** No mention.

f. **follow-up** The State Department of Health shall follow-up affected children and inform guardians of procedures for detection, prevention, and treatment. § 34-24-24 (1977)

g. **education** The department shall provide for an education program among physicians, staffs of hospitals, public health nurses, and the public. § 34-24-16 (Supp. 1984)

h. **counseling** No mention.

i. **research** No mention.

j. **other** According to a 1983 communication from the department of health, the department "receives tests results on all children screened to match against birth certificates."

2. **Are there confidentiality requirements?** No mention.

3. **Is a registry established?** No mention.

C. **For the costs of the program?** No mention.

V. **Are there sanctions to punish non-compliance?** No mention.

TENNESSEE

I. **Is there a statute addressing neonatal genetic screening?** Tenn. Code Ann. § 68-5-301 et seq. (1983). Regulations are set forth in Rules of Tennessee Department of Public Health Bureau of Community Health Services Administration. § 1200-15-1-.01 to -.07 (1982)

A. **Does it state an objective?** To prevent mental retardation. § 68-5-301

B. **Does it compel screening?** Mandatory. § 68-5-301

1. **Are there exceptions?** Parents may object if they are members of a well-organized church or religious denomination which opposes medical treatment for diseases or physical defects. § 68-5-308

2. **Does it provide notice to parents and guardians of the right to object?** No mention.

II. **What does the program screen for and how readily can other tests be added?** Phenylketonuria, hypothyroidism, and other metabolic disorders and defects likely to cause mental retardation. § 68-5-301, 302

III. **Does the statute provide for centralization or quality assurance?** Testing and reporting of results shall be done at such times, places, and manner as the Public Health Council prescribes. § 68-5-304 The regulations require that specimens be sent to the Division of Laboratories of the Department of Public Health. § 1200-15-1-.02(a)

IV. **Who is responsible . . .**

A. **For each individual screen?** The commissioner of public health shall designate the person(s) to be charged with the duty to cause screening, which may include: the person required to file a birth certificate, the parents, guardian or custodian during its first two weeks of life, or such other person(s) as the commissioner deems appropriate. § 68-5-303 The regulations state that it is the responsibility of the chief administrative officer of a hospital and the attending physician to see that a blood specimen is submitted to the department Division of Laboratories. § 1200-15-1-.02(1)(a) If an infant is screened earlier than 48 hours after birth, the administrative officer and attending physician should direct the parents to have the child retested for phenylketonuria and hypothyroidism before it is two weeks old. § 1200-15-1-.02(1)(b) Parents who are new residents are responsible for having an infant tested before it is two weeks old unless there is proof of previous testing. § 1200-15-1-.02(1)(c) According to the regulations in the case of an infant tested at discharge prior to 48 hours after birth, it is the responsibility of the chief administrative officer of the hospital of the infant's birth to provide the parents with a pamphlet setting out the requirements of the department for repeat testing. § 1200-15-1-.03

B. **For the program?** The Public Health Council (§ 68-5-302) and the state Department of Public Health (§ 68-5-303), which shall promulgate rules and regulations.

1. **Does the program provide for . . .**

   a. **testing** The public health council shall promulgate rules regarding tests and examinations in accordance with accredited medical practices. § 68-5-302 The Department of Public Health shall promulgate rules for obtaining, handling and delivering samples. § 68-5-303 The rules require that a blood specimen (original or repeat if the original was collected prior to 48 hours after birth) be collected before two weeks of age. § 1200-15-1-.02(1)(d)

   b. **confirming positive result** The State Department of Public Health shall do or require testing to confirm positive results. § 68-5-305 According to the regulations, "[e]ach local health department shall assist the State Department of Public Health in contacting all cases suspected of having phenylketonuria to confirm or disprove the presumptive screening result based on the Guthrie Test, and all suspected of having hypothyroidism to disprove the presumptive screening result based on the T_4 and TSH tests." § 1200-15-1-.04

   c. **reporting** Reporting of results shall be done at such times, places, and in such a manner as prescribed by the department. § 68-5-304

   d. **recording** No mention.

   e. **treatment** No mention.

   f. **follow-up** No mention.

   g. **education** The department shall furnish health professionals with medical information. § 68-5-306 The public shall be extensively informed as to the nature and effects of metabolic disorders. § 68-5-301

   h. **counseling** No mention.

   i. **research** No mention.

j. other This statute mandates interdepartmental cooperation in carrying out this act. § 68-5-307 The department shall report to the governor and the legislature during each session as to the progress and effect of the testing programs. § 68-5-310

2. Are there confidentiality requirements? No mention.

3. Is a registry established? No mention.

C. For the costs of the program? No mention.

V. Are there sanctions to punish non-compliance? Willful refusal or failure to have a child tested is a misdemeanor. § 68-5-309

TEXAS

I. **Is there a statute addressing neonatal genetic screening?** Tex. Rev. Civ. Stat. Ann. art. 4447e § 1 et seq. and e-1 § 1 et seq. (Vernon Supp. 1984). Regulations governing the testing procedure are established in Texas Department of Health Maternal and Child Health Services "Testing Newborn Children for Phenylketonuria, Other Heritable Diseases, and Hypothyroidism" § 37.51 to 37.61 (1983).

A. **Does it state an objective?** To combat mental retardation. 4447e § 1

B. **Does it compel screening?** Mandatory. 4447e § 2 and 4447e-1 § 3

1. **Are there exceptions?** Parents may object on religious grounds. 4447e § 2 and 4447e-1 § 5; § 37.53(a) (regulations) The regulations provide for an additional exception: the delay of testing due to medical considerations. § 37.53

2. **Does it provide notice to parents and guardians of the right to object?** No mention.

II. **What does the program screen for and how readily can other tests be added?** Phenylketonuria and other heritable diseases specified by the board (4447e § 1) and hypothyroidism (4447e-1 § 1). The regulations provide for testing for phenylketonuria, galactosemia, hypothyroidism, and sickling hemoglobinopathies. § 37.55

III. **Does the statute provide for centralization or quality assurance?** The Department of Health shall establish and maintain a diagnostic laboratory to develop tests and such other purposes considered necessary by the department 4447e § 1. The test must be performed either in the department's diagnostic laboratory or by an approved laboratory. 4447e § 2 and 4447e-1 § 2 Procedures for approving a laboratory are set forth in 4447e § 2A and 4447e-1 § 4. Nevertheless, the regulations provide for all tests to be performed by the department. § 37.56

IV. **Who is responsible . . .**

A. **For each individual screen?** The physician attending a newborn or the person attending a newborn not attended by a physician. 4447e § 2 and 4447e-1 § 3

B. **For the program?** The Department of Health establishes, maintains and carries out the program and the Board of Health adopts regulations governing the program. 4447e § 1

1. **Does the program provide for . . .**

a. **testing** The Texas Department of Health shall specify the heritable diseases covered. 4447e § 1 Specific instructions regarding the methods and timing of testing are set forth in the regulations (§§ 37.55, 37.56) including mandatory phenylketonuria retesting of all infants discharged prior to 24 hours after protein feeding was started. (§ 37.55(a)) and recommended six month confirmatory studies when sickling hemoglobinopathies are abnormal (§ 37.55(b)).

b. **confirming positive result** No mention in the statutes of how tests should be confirmed.

c. **reporting** The statutes imply that the attending physician should notify a city or county health officer. 4447e § 2, 4447e-1 § 6. According to the regulations, laboratory results will be mailed to the person specified on the screening form upon completion of testing by the department. § 37.55 The regulations also provide that individuals must report to the department all confirmed cases detected through mechanisms other than the newborn screening program.

d. **recording** No mention.

e. **treatment** Upon confirmation of a positive result, the department shall supply services and facilities to the family and the physician to the extent necessary and, where necessary or desirable, provide for care and treatment of affected children. 4447e § 2 When a positive test for hypothyroidism is confirmed, state services shall be made available to establish a definitive diagnosis and to supervise treatment. § 4447e-1 § 7

f. **follow-up** The Department may follow-up positive tests with the attending physician, the attending physician's designee, the city or county health officer, or the parents of the newborn child. § 4447e § 2 The city or county health officer shall follow-up all positive tests with the attending physician. 4447e § 2 and 4447e-1 § 6 The regulations provide that the department will maintain an active system of follow-up. (§ 37.59(a)) and that the person attending the newborn is responsible for assisting "in the provision of follow-up to confirmed cases, when appropriate" (§ 37.59(a)). They also state that local or regional health departments will provide follow-up. § 37.59(b)

g. **education** No mention.

h. **counseling** No mention.

i. **research** The department shall establish a laboratory for conducting experiments and projects necessary to develop ways and means to prevent and treat heritable diseases in children. 4447e § 1, 4447e-1 § 1 The regulations provide for data collection to derive incidence/prevalence rates. § 37.59(d)

2. **Are there confidentiality requirements?** No mention.

3. **Is a registry established?** No mention in the statutes. According to the regulations "data will be collected in order to derive incidence/prevalence rates for the various conditions." .015(d)

C. **For the costs of the program?** No mention. However, the provisions covering hypothyroidism screening provide that "[t]he department may receive gifts and donations on behalf of the program." 4447e-1 § 10

V. **Are there sanctions to punish non-compliance?** No mention. No physician, technician, or person giving tests will be liable because the parent did not consent to testing. 4447e § 2, 4447e-1 § 5

UTAH

I. **Is there a statute addressing neonatal genetic screening?** Utah Code Ann. § 26-17-21 (1976) and § 26-10-6 (Supp. 1981). The Department of Social Services State Division of Health has adopted "Rules and Regulations Pertaining to Testing of Newborn Infants for Phenylketonuria and Other Metabolic Diseases Which May Result in Mental Retardation or Brain Damage" (1978).

A. **Does it state an objective?** No specific mention, but the implied goal is to prevent and treat such metabolic diseases which may result in mental retardation. § 26-10-6

B. **Does it compel screening?** Mandatory. § 26-10-6.

1. **Are there exceptions?** Parents who are members of a well-recognized religious organization may object if testing is contrary to the religious organization's teachings. § 26-10-6

2. **Does it provide notice to parents and guardians of the right to object?** No mention.

II. **What does the program screen for and how readily can other tests be added?** Phenylketonuria and other metabolic diseases which cause mental retardation or brain damage and for which a preventive measure or treatment is available and a reliable laboratory exists. § 26-10-6 The regulations provide for screening for phenylketonuria, congenital hypothroidism, galactosemia and other metabolic diseases. § I

III. **Does the statute provide for centralization or quality assurance?** No mention in the statute. According to the regulations, a blood sample and required information should be sent in a preaddressed kit supplied by the Division of Health. § IIIC

IV. **Who is responsible . . .**

A. **For each individual screen?** No mention in the statute. The regulations give responsibility for the first screening to the hospital and the physician or other person responsible for signing the birth certificate. § III(A) and (B) The parents or guardian are responsible for arranging for the second screening. § III(F)

B. **For the program?** The Department of Social Services, which shall establish rules, and regulations. 26-10-6

1. **Does the program provide for . . .**
   a. **testing** The Department shall establish rules for testing. § 26-10-6 The regulations provide guidelines for testing (§ III and § IV), including samples to be taken from each infant before discharge and between two and four weeks of age.
   b. **confirming positive result** No mention.
   c. **reporting** No mention.
   d. **recording** No mention.
   e. **treatment** No mention.
   f. **follow-up** Under the regulations, the parents or guardian of an infant with a positive or questionable test result shall promptly refer the infant to a physician for quantitative evaluation of the metabolic problem. § IV(D) The physician in turn must obtain the final diagnosis and notify the Division of Health within 14 days after referral. § IV(E)
   g. **education** No mention.
   h. **counseling** No mention.
   i. **research** No mention.
   j. **other** According to § 26-10-(2)(a), the crippled children's service includes early location of crippled children, provided that any prenatal diagnosis "not be used for screening, but rather will be utilized only when there are medical or genetic indications which warrant diagnosis."
2. **Are there confidentiality requirements?** No mention.
3. **Is a registry established?** No mention.

C. **For the costs of the program?** The department may charge a fee for tests sufficient to cover laboratory costs and follow-up. § 26-10-6 The regulations provide that the fee charged shall be retained by the Division of Health to offset the cost of the program. § V

V. **Are there sanctions to punish non-compliance?** No mention.

VERMONT

1. Is there a statute addressing neonatal genetic screening? No.

VIRGINIA

I. **Is there a statute addressing neonatal genetic screening?** Va. Code § 32.1-65 et seq. (1982 and Supp. 1984). There are "Rules and Regulations of the Board of Health Commonwealth of Virginia Governing the Detection and Control of Phenylketonuria," amended April 1, 1982.

A. **Does it state an objective?** To prevent mental retardation. § 32.1-65 (Supp. 1983)

B. **Does it compel screening?** Mandatory (§ 32.1-65 (Supp. 1984)) except that the sickle cell testing is voluntary (§ 32.1-68(A)).

1. **Are there exceptions?** Parents may object on religious grounds. § 32.1-65 (Supp. 1984); § 3.01 (regulation)

2. **Does it provide notice to parents and guardians of the right to object?** No mention.

II. **What does the program screen for and how readily can other tests be added?** Phenylketonuria, maple syrup urine disease, hypothyroidism, galactosemia, homocystinuria (§ 32.1-65 (Supp. 1984)) and other genetically related diseases and genetic traits and inborn errors of metabolism, including sickle cell anemia (§ 32.1-68(A) (1982)).

III. **Does the statute provide for centralization or quality assurance?** The statute provides that the Division of Consolidated Laboratory Services shall perform the tests. § 32.1-72 The regulations provide that the specimen may be mailed to Division of Consolidated Laboratory Services or to a private laboratory. § 3.04.01

IV. **Who is responsible . . .**

A. **For each individual screen?** The physician, nurse or midwife in charge of the delivery of a baby or, if none, the first attending physician. § 32.1-65 (Supp. 1984); § 3.03 (regulation)

B. **For the program?** The statutes do not specify who has responsibility for the mandatory newborn screening program. They do provide that the Commissioner of Health, in cooperation with local health directors, shall establish the program for voluntary screening of sickle cell anemia. § 32.1-68 (1982) They also provide that the Board of Health shall recommend procedures for treatment of phenylketonuria. § 32.1-67 (Supp. 1984)

1. **Does the program provide for . . .**
   a. **testing** The Board shall determine the method of screening. § 32-1-68(B) (1982). The regulations cover the timing of the testing. (§§ 3.02, 3.03)
   b. **confirming positive result** The Commissioner is to notify attending physician of a suspicion of phenylketonuria and the need for additional testing to confirm or disprove the diagnosis. § 32.1-66 Under the regulations, the Director of the Bureau of Maternal and Child Health notifies the attending physician or local health director, as appropriate, to arrange further evaluation. § 4.03.
   c. **reporting** All physicians, public health nurses, and hospital administrators shall report the discovery of cases of phenylketonuria to the commissioner. § 32.1-66 (1982) The screening results shall be sent to the physician if known and either to the parents when the person screened is under the age of eighteen or to the person if he is over 18. § 32.1-69 (1982)
   d. **recording** No mention.
   e. **treatment** The Board shall recommend procedures for treatment of phenylketonuria and provide it for medically indigent families, including special food products. § 32.1-67 (Supp. 1984) Under the regulations, the Director of the Bureau of Maternal and Child Health provides the services of a phenylketonuria team (§ 5.01) and recommends to the attending physician that the patient be evaluated and treated by the combined efforts of a physician trained in treating inborn errors of metabolism, a nutritionist, and a public health nurse (§ 4.03).
   f. **follow-up** No mention in the statute.
   g. **education** Commissioner to establish screening programs which provide for education and post-screening counseling for those affected with sickle cell anemia and other genetically related diseases and inborn errors of metabolism. § 32.1-68 (1982)
   h. **counseling** The commissioner is authorized to establish programs for post-screening counseling. § 32.1-68 (1982)
   i. **research** No mention.
2. **Are there confidentiality requirements?** All records maintained as part of any screening program shall be strictly confidential. The results may be used for research and collective statistical purposes. § 32.1-69 (1982)

a. **Who has access?** The Board, the Commissioner or his agents or to the local health director and others by explicit permission of the person over age 18 or the parents if the person is under age 18. § 32.1-69 (1982)

3. **Is a registry established?** No mention.

C. **For the costs of the program?** Laboratory tests shall be made without charge. § 32.1-72 (1982) The regulations provide that the test itself, and the supplies to collect and transport the specimen, shall be provided by the Department without charge. § 3.04.02 Treatment of phenylketonuria shall be provided for medically indigent families. § 32.1-67 (Supp. 1984); § 5.02 (regulation) Parents of an affected child shall, in the discretion of the department, reimburse the local health department for the cost of special food products for treating phenylketonuria in an amount not to exceed 2% of their gross income. § 32.1-67 (Supp. 1984)

V. **Are there sanctions to punish non-compliance?** The failure of any physician, nurse, or midwife to comply shall, in addition to any other penalty prescribed by law, constitute grounds for revocation of the license or permit by the issuing board. § 32.1-73 (1982); § 6.01 (regulation)

WASHINGTON

I. **Is there a statute addressing neonatal genetic screening?** Wash. Rev. Code Ann. § 70.83.010 et seq. (West 1978 and Supp. 1982). The regulations are set forth in Wash. Admin. Code R. 248-29-050 et seq. and R. 248-102-010 et seq (1980).

A. **Does it state an objective?** To detect as early as feasible and prevent where possible preventable heritable disorders leading to mental retardation or physical defects. § 70.83.010

B. **Does it compel screening?** Mandatory. § 70.83.020

1. **Are there exceptions?** Parents may object on religious grounds. § 70.83.020 The regulations provide that a refusal signed by the parents be sent to the genetics program by a birth center. R. 248-29-050(11)(d) Other regulations covering hospital births similiarly require a written statement obtained by hospital staff be sent to the Health Services Division in lieu of the specimen for the newborn. R. 248-102-020(2)

2. **Does it provide notice to parents and guardians of the right to object?** No mention in the statute. According to the regulations, hospital personnel shall inform parents or guardians that a blood sample is to be taken from the infant in compliance with state law. R. 248-102-020(2) In birth centers, "[e]ducational materials shall be provided to each client relative to metabolic screening and informed consent for metabolic screening." R. 248-29-050(11)(a)

II. **What does the program screen for and how readily can other tests be added?** Phenylketonuria and other heritable or metabolic disorders specified by the Board of Health. § 70.83.020 The regulations cover screening for phenylketonuria and hypothyroidism. R. 248-102-020

III. **Does the statute provide for centralization or quality assurance?** The state Department of Social and Health Services shall offer the use of its services and facilities. § 70.83.040 The regulations require samples to be sent to the Health Services Division Laboratory. R. 248-102-020

IV. **Who is responsible . . .**

A. For each individual screen? The statute is not explicit. According to the regulations, administrators of hospitals and maternity care centers. R. 248-102-020

B. For the program? The Department of Social and Health Services. §§ 70.83.020, 030 The State Board of Health shall promulgate rules and regulations. § 70.83.050 (1978)

1. **Does the program provide for . . .**

   a. **testing** The regulations set forth guidelines for the timing of testing and provide that specimens must be collected prior to discharge or by 10 days if undischarged and must be sent by the next working day to the Health Services Division Laboratory. R. 248-102-020

   b. **confirming positive result** No mention in the statute. The regulations state that a presumptive positive "will not constitute a final laboratory or medical diagnosis." The attending physician is notified, or, if there is none, the family. R. 248-102-040(2) The department offers assistance in arranging further diagnosis. R. 248-102-040(3)

   c. **reporting** All positive tests shall be reported by laboratories, attending physicians, hospital administrators or others performing or requesting the tests to the Department of Social and Health Services. § 70.83.030 The regulations require that the department which performs the initial laboratory testing promptly notify the attending physician or the family if a presumptive positive result is obtained and help to arrange for further testing. R. 248-102-040 (2) (3)

   d. **recording** No mention in the statute. The regulations provide that the birth center maintain a health record for each maternal and newborn client which documents that the screening specimen was obtained. R. 248-29-070(2)(b)

   e. **treatment** When notified of a positive test, the department shall offer the use of its services and facilities. § 70.83.040

   f. **follow-up** No mention.

   g. **education** No mention.

   h. **counseling** No mention.

   i. **research** No mention.

   j. **other** The regulations require the establishment of a mechanism for weekly reporting of all live births to the genetics program. R. 248-29-050(11)(b)

2. **Are there confidentiality requirements?** No mention in the statute. The regulations establish a confidentiality requirement for birth center records. R. 248-29-070 (1).

3. **Is a registry established?** No mention.

C. **For the costs of the program?** The services and facilities of the department and cooperating agencies will be made available to the families so required. § 70.83.040 According to the regulations, both the department and the hospital are authorized to make a reasonable charge to the parents. R. 248-102-070 Financial support for follow-up diagnosis is available to qualified families. R. 248-102-040 (3)

V. **Are there sanctions to punish non-compliance?** No mention.

WEST VIRGINIA

I. Is there a statute addressing neonatal genetic screening? W. Va. Code § 16-22-1 et seq. (Supp. 1983).

A. Does it state an objective? To lessen or prevent the suffering of those affected by genetic defects affecting body metabolism through early detection and treatment. § 16-22-1

B. Does it compel screening? Mandatory. § 16-22-3.

1. Are there exceptions? No mention.

2. Does it provide notice to parents and guardians of the right to object? No mention.

II. What does the program screen for and how readily can other tests be added? Phenylketonuria, galactosemia, hypothyroidism. § 16-22-3

III. Does the statute provide for centralization or quality assurance? The Department of Health shall establish and maintain facilities at its state hygienic laboratory and may establish additional laboratories. § 16-22-2

IV. Who is responsible . . .

A. For each individual screen? The physician attending a newborn or any person attending a newborn not under the care of a physician. § 16-22-3.

B. For the program? The state Department of Health is authorized to establish and carry out a program and to adopt necessary rules and regulations. § 16-22-2

1. Does the program provide for . . .

a. testing Tests by the state laboratory shall be made upon request by physicians, hospital medical personnel and other authorized individuals attending newborns. § 16-22-2 No specific guidelines are mentioned.

b. confirming positive result No mention.

c. reporting Any test found positive shall be promptly reported to the department by the laboratory director. § 16-22-3

d. recording No mention.

e. treatment The State Department of Health in cooperation with other state departments and agencies, and with attending physicians, may provide medical, dietary, and related assistance to affected infants. § 16-22-3

f. **follow-up** No mention.

g. **education** No mention.

h. **counseling** No mention.

i. **research** No mention.

2. **Are there confidentiality requirements?** No mention.

3. **Is a registry established?** No mention.

C. **For the costs of the program?** No mention.

V. **Are there sanctions to punish non-compliance?** No mention.

WISCONSIN

I. **Is there a statute addressing neonatal genetic screening?** Wis. Stat. Ann. § 146.02 (West Supp. 1982-83).

A. **Does it state an objective?** No mention.

B. **Does it compel screening?** Every infant shall be subjected to a blood test § 146.02(1), but urine tests are voluntary. § 146.02(1m).

1. **Are there exceptions?** Parents or legal guardian may object on religious grounds. § 146.02(3)

2. **Does it provide notice to parents and guardians of the right to object?** No tests may be performed unless the parents or legal guardian are fully informed of the purposes of testing and have been given reasonable opportunity to object. § 146.02(3)

II. **What does the program screen for and how readily can other tests be added?** Phenylketonuria, galactosemia, maple syrup urine disease, hypothyroidism, and other metabolic disorders as the Department of Public Health directs. § 146.02(1)

III. **Does the statute provide for centralization or quality assurance?** Tests are performed in such laboratories as the department approves. In approving laboratories, the department shall take into consideration the costs of testing under the the alternative options of using: (a) a single lab; (b) several laboratories on a geographic or other basis; (c) all laboratories, public and private. § 146.02(2)

IV. **Who is responsible . . .**

A. **For each individual screen?** The attending physician for each infant born in a hospital or maternity home prior to discharge. § 146.02(1)

B. **For the program?** The Department of Public Health, which may adopt rules and regulations. § 146.02(2)

1. **Does the program provide for . . .**

a. **testing** The department shall prescribe which tests should be performed, rules for tests to be performed, and which laboratories will perform the tests. § 146.02(2)

b. **confirming positive result** No mention.

c. **reporting** Test results are reported by the laboratory to the physician, who advises the parents or guardian of the results. § 146.02(4)

d. **recording** No mention.

e. **treatment** No mention.

f. **follow-up** No mention.

g. **education** No mention.

h. **counseling** No mention.

i. **research** No mention.

j. **other** The department may compile data for statistical analysis § 146.02(4).

2. **Are there confidentiality requirements?** No information may be disclosed without parental consent except for data compiled by the department without reference to the identity of any individual. § 146.02(4)

a. **Who has access?** No mention.

3. **Is a registry established?** No mention.

C. **For the costs of the program?** No mention.

V. **Are there sanctions to punish non-compliance?** No mention.

WYOMING

I. Is there a statute addressing neonatal genetic screening? Wyo. Stat. § 35-4-801 (Supp. 1983). The Department of Health and Social Services has adopted regulations, "Mandatory Screening of Newborn Infants for Inborn Errors of Metabolism," Chapter 35.

A. Does it state an objective? No mention.

B. Does it compel screening? Mandatory. § 35-4-801(a).

1. Are there exceptions? Any objection by the parent or guardian will exempt a child. § 35-4-801(c) The regulations provide that the refusal be in writing. § 3

2. Does it provide notice to parents and guardians of the right to object? Informed consent of parents shall be obtained. § 35-4-801(c) The regulations provide that written consent is necessary. § 3

II. What does the program screen for and how readily can other tests be added? Remedial inborn errors of metabolism. § 35-4-801(a). The regulations specify that testing be done for phenylketonuria, hypothyroidism, galactosemia, homocystinuria, maple syrup urine disease, sickle cell anemia and other diseases caused by inborn errors of metabolism specified by the designated committee. § 2

III. Does the statute provide for centralization or quality assurance? No mention in the statute. The regulations state that blood samples shall be sent to "the regional laboratory." § 4(c)

IV. Who is responsible . . .

A. For each individual screen? No mention in the statute. The regulations provide that if a child is born outside of a hospital, the birth attendant shall arrange for the sample to be taken. § 4(b)

B. For the program? The state Department of Health and Social Services, Division of Health and Medical Services, which may adopt regulations. § 35-4-801(a)

1. Does the program provide for . . .

a. testing The division shall prescribe the manner of screening. § 35-4-801(a) The specific tests to be done shall be determined by a committee of the division's administrator, the Wyoming state medical society president, and members of the Wyoming state pediatric society and the

Wyoming obstetric/gynecological society. § 35-4-801(b) The screening shall take place 3 to 5 days after natural childbirth or 5 to 8 days after a premature birth. § 35-4-801(a) The regulations specify the timing of the testing and provide that samples be sent to the regional laboratory within 24 hours of collection. § 4 They also provide that a follow-up phenylketonuria test be collected when the infant is two weeks of age. § 5

b. **confirming positive result** No mention.

c. **reporting** No mention in the statute. The regulations require that positive or questionable results be reported to the infant's physician as well as to the Division. § 5

d. **recording** No mention in the statute. The regulations require hospitals to maintain a record of the numbers of births and numbers of infants tested which includes the number of infants not tested and the reasons why. § 4(d)

e. **treatment** No mention.

f. **follow-up** No mention.

g. **education** No mention.

h. **counseling** No mention.

i. **research** No mention.

2. **Are there confidentiality requirements?** No mention in the statute. The regulations of the division, in their statement on confidentiality of medical records, provide that medical records are confidential and shall not be released except on court order or written consent of the patient.

3. **Is a registry established?** No mention.

C. **For the costs of the program?** No mention.

V. **Are there sanctions to punish non-compliance?** No mention.

Appendices

Sickle Cell Screening Laws and Regulations

By Lori B. Andrews

Research Attorney and Project Director, American Bar Foundation

Enacted in the early 1970s, the first sickle cell screening laws evolved out of a social and political climate influenced by the civil rights movement and a heightened awareness of social inequalities.[1] The first state law appeared in Massachusetts in July 1971[2] and by the end of 1972, screening laws had been passed in twelve states and the District of Columbia. Criticism of these laws arose almost simultaneously, and reflected a growing public discussion of the risks and benefits of programs aimed at testing for sickle cell trait. The public criticism of these laws focused on the problem of stigmatization of and discrimination against carriers of sickle cell trait. The concerns were both that carriers of sickle cell trait would be discriminated against in employment opportunities and insurance coverage and that the screening laws provided a logic for controlling the reproductive behavior of black persons and therefore hinted at the possibility of genocide.[3]

The fear that state-authorized sickle cell screening might provide a source of discrimination was not unfounded. In a paper delivered in 1972 at the National Conference on the Mental Health Aspects of Sickle Cell Anemia, Dr. James Bowman detailed some of the actual incidents of what he called "genetic discrimination" which he maintained were engendered by screening legislation. These included the grounding of black airline employees who were carriers because of a concern that they might go into a sickling crises if the plane depressurized. In addition, insurance companies charged higher rates for carriers of sickle cell trait without substantial evidence that possession of sickle cell trait placed a person at a significantly higher risk of death or illness. And the armed forces considered deferment of sickle cell trait carriers, thereby potentially foreclosing on substantial employment opportunities for some blacks.[4]

These types of discrimination were fostered by a general misunderstanding of the nature of sickle cell anemia--a misunderstaning embodied in the language as well as in the provisions of the early laws. Though sickle cell anemia is a devastating

1. The following discussion of the initial sickle cell screening laws is based on Philip Reilly's Genetics, Law and Social Policy 62-86 (1977).

2. Comment, "Constitutional and Practical Considerations in Mandatory Sickle Cell Anemia Testing," 7 U.C. Davis L. Rev. 509, 512 (1974).

3. Id. at 67.

4. Id. at 74, citing J. E. Bowman, "Sickle Cell Screening: Medico-legal, Ethical, Psychological and Social Problems: A Sickle Cell Crisis." Paper presented at Meharry Medical College (1972, unpublished).

disease, the possession of sickle cell trait generally has no constraining effects. Unfortunately the early statutes embodied scientific errors which helped to further a misunderstanding about the nature of sickle cell anemia. The laws often tended to identify carrier status with affliction of the disease, and thereby fostered the erroneous notion that carriers of sickle cell trait were afflicted with a debilitating health condition. As Philip Reilly observes, "they [the early laws] are a sad commentary on the abyss that separates lawmakers from technical experts."[5]

Not only did the language of these statutes reflect a misunderstanding of the nature of sickle cell anemia, many of their provisions concerning the timing and situations for testing provided a confusing picture of the purposes of sickle cell screening. If the principle aim of these statutes was to enable the identification of carriers of sickle cell trait so that they may be informed of their risk of producing an afflicted child, the testing programs authorized by statute seemed inconsistent with this purpose. For example, several of these laws required the testing of children prior to entering school. Yet if the intent is to identify sickle cell carriers who might risk bearing afflicted children, testing six year olds appears to be of little value, since they are not likely to be bearing children and their parents might not remember to inform them of the testing results in later years.

Aside from fostering the stigmatization of black persons in general and carriers of the sickle trait in particular, the state laws failed to achieve their purported aims in several important ways. Most of the early laws lacked provisions for counseling persons with sickle cell trait. Reilly notes that only four of the original 13 statutes included provisions for counseling carriers.[6] Since achieving the goal of these laws depended on carriers receiving proper information about their reproductive risks, this oversight seems especially objectionable. Furthermore, as physicians noted at the time, identifying sickle cell trait in a person without explaining its implications can lead to misunderstanding and unwarranted anxiety. Carriers need to hear that they themselves are not the subjects of sickle cell anemia.[7]

The laws also failed to provide for the education of the public about the nature of sickle cell anemia. Consequently they fostered misunderstandings about the health risk of carriers which could be used to support discriminatory practices.

Another deficiency in these laws lay in their lack of provisions for the confidentiality of genetic screening data. Very few established any means of protecting the privacy of screenees by limiting access to testing data.

5. Id. at 67.

6. Id. at 76.

7. Id. at 77.

Current Laws Addressing Sickle Cell Anemia

Since the initial passage of state statutes governing screening for sickle cell anemia and the subsequent criticism of those laws, some state legislatures have revised their statutory approaches to such screening. Laws have been repealed or revised, leaving in place a skeletal approach to the issue. Most mandatory screening laws have been abolished. The sickle cell anemia laws currently on the books vary widely from state to state, particularly in their provisions for who may be tested for sickle cell trait and at what age such testing occurs.

Statutes Authorizing General Screening Programs

Some statutes give the health department general authority to develop and operate sickle cell anemia programs[8]--such as programs for diagnosis, care and treatment of affected children and adults.[9] In one state, sickle cell screening and education programs are the responsibility of a Birth Defects Institute.[10] In an additional state, a Council on Sickle Cell Anemia is established to assess the need for programs, research, centers, and organizations targeted to this disorder.[11] That same state authorizes pilot programs for education, voluntary testing and counseling for sickle cell anemia.[12] In other states, laws giving an administrative agency or commission authority to conduct programs regarding hereditary disorders would allow for the establishment of sickle cell anemia programs.[13]

Target Population for Screening

Other state statutes are more specific, authorizing screening for a particular group--such as newborns, school children, people of reproductive age, people applying for marriage licenses, or pregnant women. Forty-eight states have statutes authorizing newborn screening for certain specified inborn errors of metabolism[14] and the language of some of these statutes is broad enough to allow state departments of health to undertake sickle cell screening on infants. In four states, for example,

8. **Kan.** Stat. Ann. §65-1, 105(a) (1980) (authority to establish statewide sickle cell testing and counseling without charge); **La.** Rev. Stat. Ann. §40.1299 (West Supp. 1984); and **Ohio** Rev. Code Ann. §3701.131 (Baldwin 1982).

9. **Ariz.** Rev. Stat. Ann. §36-797.43 and 44 (Supp. 1983); and **Ind.** Code Ann. §16-2-5-2 (1983).

10. **Iowa** §136.A2 (West Supp. 1984-1985).

11. **N.C.** Gen. Stat. §143B-192 (1983).

12. **N.C.** Gen. Stat. §143B-194 (1983).

13. See, e.g., **Md.** Pub. Health Code §13-109 (1982).

14. See "The Reach and Substance of State Newborn Screening Laws," this volume.

the newborn screening statutes authorize screening for heritable disorders[15] or other handicapping conditions[16] as the department sees fit.[17] If sickle cell anemia screening is undertaken in these states under the general authorization for newborn screening, it will be subject to the same statutory requirements as screening for metabolic disorders. In one of those four states, there is an exemption allowing for parental refusal on religious grounds.[18] In two states, parents may refuse newborn screening on any grounds.[19]

The statutes[20] or regulations[21] of seven additional states explicitly name sickle cell anemia as a screened for disorder in a newborn program. The other newborn screening rules for the state generally apply, with testing being mandatory, and with provisions for parental refusal based on religious grounds in three states[22] and on any grounds in four states.[23] One state, however, recognizes the sensitive nature of sickle cell anemia screening. Although it makes other newborn screening mandatory with a religious exception,[24] it provides that sickle cell anemia screening is strictly voluntary.[25]

The issue of which infants are to be tested is specifically addressed in Georgia, which limits newborn sickle cell testing to infants who are susceptible to or likely to have sickle cell anemia.[26] In newborn screening programs for sickle cell anemia without such a provision, presumably all newborns must be tested for the disorder, even though the incidence of the trait and the disease is much higher among blacks.

15. **Alaska** Stat. §18.15.200 (1981); **Fla.** Stat. Ann. §383.14(1) (West Supp. 1984); and **Wash.** Rev. Code Ann. §70.83.020 (West Supp. 1982).

16. **Mich.** Comp. Laws Ann. §333.5431 (West 1980) (mandatory screening).

17. Similarly, the Ohio newborn screening law authorizes the testing of newborns for "other genetic disorders" if disorder is treatable and the same sample can be used as is used for testing for phenylketonuria, homocystinuria, galactosemia and hypothyroidism. **Ohio** Rev. Code Ann. §3701.501(A) (1) and (2) (Baldwin 1984). Parents may object on religious grounds. Id. at §3701.502 (Baldwin 1984).

18. **Wash.** Rev. Code Ann. §70.83.020 (West Supp. 1982).

19. **Alaska** Stat. §18.15.200(f); and **Fla.** Stat. Ann. §383.14(3) (West Supp. 1984).

20. **Colo.** Rev. Stat. §25-4-1004 (1983); **Ga.** Stat. Ann. §88-1201.1(a) (Supp. 1984); **La.** Rev. Stat. Ann. §40.1299.1 (West Supp. 1984); and **N.Y.** Pub. Health Law §2500-a(a) (McKinney 1972).

21. **N.M.** Health and Environment Dept., "Newborn Screening Program Regulations" §103(B); **Tx.** Dept. of Health, Maternal and Child Health Services, "Testing Newborn Children for Phenylketonuria, Other Heritable Diseases, and Hypothyroidism" §37.55 (1983); and **Wyo.** Dept. of Health and Social Services, "Mandatory Screening of Newborn Infants for Inborn Errors of Metabolism" ch. 35 §2.

22. **Ga.** Stat. Ann. §88-1201.1(a) (Supp. 1983); **N.Y.** Pub. Health Law §2500-a(b) (McKinney 1972); and **Tx.** Rev. Civ. Stat. Ann. §4447e §2 (Vernon Supp. 1984).

23. **Colo.** Rev. Stat. §25-4-1005 (1983); **La.** Rev. Stat. Ann. §40.1299.1 (West Supp. 1984); **N.M.** Stat. Ann. §24-1-6(A), (D) (Supp. 1982); and **Wyo.** Stat. §35-4-801 (Supp. 1983).

24. **Va.** Code §32.1-65 (Supp. 1984).

25. **Va.** Code §32.1-68(A) (1982).

26. **Ga.** Ann. Code §88-1201.1(a) (Supp. 1984).

Various statutes address the screening of school age children. These laws differ in who has the discretion to initiate screening and what mechanisms exist for parental objection to screening. In Louisiana, a child entering school must present evidence of having been tested for sickle cell anemia. If there is no evidence, the student is tested, unless the parent objects in writing.[27] In Massachusetts, school children are required to have a sickle cell screen if the health commissioner determines they are susceptible to the disorder,[28] although another Massachusetts statute provides that state testing for sickle cell anemia shall be voluntary.[29] Sickle cell testing is done in one state at the discretion of the health department (with parental objections allowed on religious grounds),[30] while two other states' statutes merely authorize the board of health to establish sickle cell testing programs for school age children (with no specific mention of parental refusal).[31] In another state, school children may be tested for sickle cell anemia at the discretion of the examining physician or school nurse,[32] unless the parents object in writing.[33]

The Connecticut law on the screening of school children is the most detailed. A child must have a health assessment prior to school enrollment and later in grades 6 or 7 and grades 10 or 11. The board of education has discretion for including sickle cell screening as part of that assessment.[34] Parents get written prior notice of the assessment and a chance to be present or arrange for an assessment on their own.[35] The child need not submit to the test if the parents object on religious grounds.[36]

The South Carolina statute authorizes a voluntary screening program directed entirely at individuals of reproductive age. The program includes testing, counseling, referral and basic education "so as to eradicate the stigma attached to this malady."[37]

27. **La.** Rev. Stat. Ann. §17.170(A) and (D) (West 1982).

28. **Mass.** Ann. Laws ch. 76 §15A (Michie/Law Coop. Supp. 1978).

29. **Mass.** Ann. Laws ch. 76 §15B (Michie/Law Coop. Supp. 1978).

30. **Cal.** Health and Safety Code §325(a) and (b) (West 1979).

31. **Miss.** Code Ann. §41-24-1 (1983); and **N.M.** Stat. Ann. §24-3-1(B)(2) (Supp. 1982).

32. **Ind.** Code Ann. §20-8.1-7-14 (Burns 1975).

33. **Ind.** Code Ann. §20-8.1-7-2 (Burns Supp. 1984).

34. **Conn.** Gen. Stat. Ann. §10-206(b) and (c) (West Supp. 1985).

35. **Conn.** Gen. Stat. Ann. §10-206(a) (West Supp. 1985).

36. **Conn.** Gen. Stat. Ann. §10-208 (West Supp. 1985).

37. **S.C.** Code §44-33-10 (1977).

Other states attempt to reach people of childbearing age with laws addressed to couples applying for marriage licenses. Some testing in connection with obtaining a marriage license is strictly voluntary. In Georgia, for example, the required physician's certificate shall state that the applicant has been offered sickle cell anemia testing and counseling.[38] In contrast, in Illinois, a couple who wish to forgo sickle cell testing must go to great lengths. The required medical exam for a marriage license includes a sickle cell screen if the physician determines it is necessary.[39] To waive the testing, an individual must convince a circuit court judge that the test is contrary to his or her religion and that the public health will not be adversely affected.[40] The Kentucky law leaves sickle cell testing and subsequent counseling of carriers and affected individuals up to the physician's discretion, with no provision for a waiver.[41] The New York law requires sickle cell anemia testing as may be necessary for marriage license applicants, but does not tell who determines necessity.[42] A person may refuse the test on religious grounds[43] and a positive test may not serve as the basis for the denial of a marriage license.[44]

Three states (Alabama, California, and Oregon) that have voluntary prenatal screening programs that offer amniocentesis where both parents are carriers of an autosomal recessive trait which can be detected prenatally.[45] Conceivably, this would allow for prenatal screening for sickle cell anemia. An Arizona law authorizes the health department to offer voluntary[46] testing of pregnant women specifically for sickle cell anemia.[47]

Services Other than Screening

A number of states have provisions for sickle cell services beyond testing--including research,[48] counseling,[49] and the establishment of programs for the care of people with sickle cell disease.[50]

38. **Ga.** Stat. Ann. §53-216 and 53-9909(a)(2) (1981).

39. **Ill.** Ann. Stat. ch. 40 §204 (Smith-Hurd Supp. 1984-1985).

40. **Ill.** Ann. Stat. ch. 40 §205 (Smith-Hurd Supp. 1984-1985).

41. **Ky.** Rev. Stat. §402.320 (Supp. 1982).

42. **N.Y.** Dom. Rel. Law §13-aa(1) (McKinney 1977).

43. **N.Y.** Dom. Rel. Law §13-aa(3) (McKinney 1977).

44. **N.Y.** Dom. Rel. Law §13-aa(2) (McKinney 1977).

45. **Ala.** Code §22-10A-2(d)(5) (Supp. 1983); **Cal.** Health & Safety Code §291(a)(5) (West 1979); and **Ore.** Rev. Stat. §352.058(e) (1983).

46. **Ariz.** Rev. Stat. Ann. §36-797.42(C) (1974).

47. **Ariz.** Rev. Stat. Ann. §36-797.42(A)(4) (1974).

48. **Cal.** Health and Safety Code §327 (West 1979) (the department can make grants to conduct research); and **Colo.** Rev. Stat. §23-21-203 and 204(f) (1974) (establishes a sickle cell anemia research center in the University of Colorado School of Medicine).

The quality of practitioners involved in sickle cell anemia care is of legislative concern in at least two states. Louisiana requires that its sickle cell anemia clinics provide for training for physicians and medical students.[51] In North Carolina, counseling about sickle cell anemia may be done only by persons who are adequately trained and certified practitioners.[52] Additional states provide for the education of health care practitioners about sickle cell trait and sickle cell anemia.[53] Others provide for more general education of both practitioners and the public.[54]

Prevention of Stigmatization and Discrimination Against Individuals with Sickle Cell Trait or Disease

The problems caused by the initial sickle cell screening legislation appears to have led to subsequent laws in at least a few states that are concerned with protecting the confidentiality of sickle cell records, protecting against stigmatization or interference with procreative decisions of individuals with sickle cell trait and protecting against insurance or employment discrimination.

Some states explicitly provide for confidentiality of the information in the newborn context[55] or with respect to children,[56] or for confidentiality generally.[57] However, even today, the confidentiality of information collected through sickle cell anemia screening is not adequately safeguarded under most statutes. In Connecticut, although there is a statute stating that the records shall not be open to public inspection,[58] another law provides that the health assessment, including any sickle

49. **Cal.** Health and Safety Code §327 (West 1979) (the department can make grants to provide counseling); **Cal.** Health and Safety Code §342(o) (West Supp. 1984) (programs established in the department may include genetic and long term psychological counseling); **Colo.** Rev. Stat. §25-4-1003(2)(c) (1983) (counseling services shall be available to persons in need, shall be nondirective and shall emphasize informing the client); **Colo.** Rev. Stat. §23-21-204(d) (1974) (the University of Colorado School of Medicine shall establish a program for counseling); **Ga.** Stat. Ann. §88-1201.1(b) (Supp. 1984); **Kan.** Stat. Ann. §65-1,105(a) (1980) (authority to establish statewide testing and counseling program); **Mass.** Ann. Laws ch. 76 §15B (Michie/Law Coop. Supp. 1978) (department shall furnish post-screening counseling); **N.C.** Gen. Stat. §143B-194 (1983); and **Va.** Code §32.1-68 (1982).

50. **Cal.** Health and Safety Code §341 (West Supp. 1984); **Colo.** Rev. Stat. §23-21-203 and §204(b) (1974) (establishes a sickle cell anemia treatment center at the University of Colorado School of Medicine); **Fla.** Stat. Ann. §402.212(2); (West Supp. 1985); **La.** Rev. Stat. Ann. §40.1299.4 (West Supp. 1984-1985) (establishes sickle cell anemia clinics in two hospitals); **Neb.** Rev. Stat. §68-1402 (1981); **N.J.** Stat. Ann. §26:5B-4(b) and (c) (West Supp. 1982-1983) (health department shall establish guidelines for treatment and referral); **N.J.** Stat. Ann. §9:14B-1 (West 1976) (covers the establishment of sickle cell anemia homes and hospitals); and **Tenn.** Code Ann. §49-7-403 (1983) (the health department shall contract with the medical college for treatment of sickle cell anemia).

51. **La.** Rev. Stat. Ann. §40.1299.4 (West Supp. 1984-1985).

52. **N.C.** Gen. Stat. §143B-196 (1983).

53. See, e.g., **N.M.** Stat. Ann. §24-3-1(B)(1) (Supp. 1982).

54. **Colo.** Rev. Stat. §23-21-204(d) and (e) (1974); **Miss.** Code Ann. §41-24-5 (1983) (the board of health is empowered to prepare and distribute educational material about sickle cell anemia and sickle cell trait); **N.J.** Stat. Ann. §26:5B-4(d) (West Supp. 1982-1983); **N.C.** Gen. Stat. §143B-196 (1983); and **Va.** Code §32.1-68 (1982).

55. **Colo.** Rev. Stat. §25-4-1003(2)(e) (1983).

56. **Cal.** Health and Safety Code §324.5 (West 1979); and **Conn.** Gen. Stat. Ann. §10-209 (West Supp. 1985).

57. **Ga.** Ann. Code §88.1202(a) (Supp. 1984); **Kan.** Stat. Ann. §65-1,106 (1980); **Md.** Pub. Health Code Ann. §31-109(c)(1) (1984); **Mass.** Gen. Laws Ann. ch. 76 §15B (West 1978); and **Va.** Code §32.1-69 (1982).

cell screening, shall be part of the child's school file.[59] Similarly, in Louisiana, the results of school children's tests are reported to the school board.[60] This does not adequately safeguard against records being used in a stigmatizing way by teachers or school administrators.

A few specific laws exhibit sensitivity to the social effects and reproductive implications of a sickle cell anemia screening program. In California, the health department is authorized to make grants to "evaluate the social consequences of the identifications of sickle cell trait carriers."[61] The Louisiana law is concerned that carriers not be coerced into not having children. It specifically states that attempts to prevent sickle cell anemia shall not include mandatory sterilization or abortion.[62]

The statutes dealing with sickle cell anemia rarely reach the issue of discrimination against individuals having sickle cell trait. Two states, however, prohibit denying an individual life insurance[63] or disability insurance[64] or charging a higher premium[65] solely because the individual has sickle cell trait.

Florida additionally has a law prohibiting mandatory sickle cell trait screening as a condition for employment, for admission to educational institutions or to determine eligibility for adoption.[66] Another Florida statute prohibits discrimination in employment against people with sickle-cell trait.[67] Similarly, a New Jersey law prohibits employment discrimination based on an "atypical cellular blood type."[68] Louisiana has the most extensive law of these type, prohibiting employers[69] and employment agencies[70] from discriminating against individuals with sickle cell trait.

58. **Conn.** Gen. Stat. Ann. §10-209 (West Supp. 1985).

59. **Conn.** Gen. Stat. Ann. §10-206(d) (West Supp. 1985).

60. **La.** Rev. Stat. Ann. §17.170(A) (West 1982).

61. **Cal.** Health and Safety Code §327 (West 1979).

62. **La.** Rev. Stat. Ann. §40.1299 (West Supp. 1984).

63. **Fla.** Stat. Ann. §626.9706(1) (West 1984); and **La.** Rev. Stat. Ann. §652.1(D) (West Supp. 1984).

64. **Fla.** Stat. Ann. §626.9707(1) (West 1984); and **La.** Rev. Stat. Ann. §652.1(D) (West Supp. 1984).

65. **Fla.** Stat. Ann. §626.9076(2) (West 1984) (life insurance); §626.9707(2) (West 1984) (disability insurance); and **La.** Rev. Stat. Ann. §652.1(D) (West Supp. 1984).

66. This same law appears in three places in the Florida statutes: **Fla.** Stat. Ann. §448.076 (West 1981); §228.201 (West Supp. 1985); and §63.043 (West Supp. 1985).

67. **Fla.** Stat. Ann. §448.075 (West 1981).

68. **N.J.** Stat. Ann. §10:5-12 (West Supp. 1982-1983).

69. **La.** Rev. Stat. Ann. §23:1002(A)(1) (West Supp. 1984-1985).

70. **La.** Rev. Stat. Ann. §23:1002(B) (West Supp. 1984-1985).

The law also prohibits employers from limiting, segregating or classifying sickle cell carriers in any way which would tend to deprive the individual of employment opportunities or would otherwise adversely affect his status as an employee.[71]

Discrimination by unions is also of concern under the Louisiana law. The statute prohibits a labor organization from excluding or expelling individuals or otherwise discriminating against them because of sickle cell trait,[72] or from limiting, classifying or segrating its membership or failing to refer a member for a job due to sickle cell trait;[73] or from attempting to cause an employer to discriminate.[74] The Louisiana law specifically provides that individuals with sickle cell anemia can bring civil suits against employers or labor organizations in order to effectuate the purposes of the anti-discrimination laws.

The Future of Sickle Cell Anemia Screening

Although the critiques of the initial sickle cell anemia screening programs led to some revisions in state statutes, current laws still need improvement. Provisions for confidentiality and counseling should be universal. The most logical goals of a sickle cell anemia screening program would seem to be the identification of affected individuals as early as possible through a newborn screening program and the provision of information to people of reproductive age through voluntary testing for carrier status and voluntary prenatal diagnosis. Provisions for screening at other points in an individual's life should be weeded out of legislation as not sufficiently supported by public policy.

71. La. Rev. Stat. Ann. §23:1002(A)(2) (West Supp. 1984-1985).

72. La. Rev. Stat. Ann. §23:1002(c)(1) (West Supp. 1984-1985).

73. La. Rev. Stat. Ann. §23:1002(c)(2) (West Supp. 1984-1985).

74. La. Rev. Stat. Ann. §23:1002(c)(3) (West Supp. 1984-1985).

Chart of Newborn Screening Laws

	PKU	Hypothyroidism	Galactosemia	Homocystinuria	Maple Syrup Urine Disease	Other Heritable Diseases
Alabama	S	S				
Alaska	S, R					S, R
Arizona	R	R	R			
Arkansas	S, R	S				
California	R	R	R	S--authorizes study to see if tests should be implemented.	S--authorizes study to see if test should be implemented.	S--authorizes study to see if tests for histidinemia and galactokinase deficiency should be implemented.
Colorado	S, R	S	S	S	S	S--abnormal hemoglobins.
Connecticut	S, R	S	S			S--other inborn errors of metabolism.
Delaware	V	V	V	V	V	
District of Columbia	S	S				S--other metabolic diseases if the mayor specifies by regulation.
Florida	S, R	R	R		R	S--other metabolic, hereditary, or congenital disorders.
Georgia	S, R	S, R	S, R	S, R	S, R	S--tyrosinemia, sickle cell anemia, other such inherited metabolic diseases.
Hawaii	S	S				
Idaho	S, R					S, R--authorizes testing for such other diseases as state board of health & welfare prescribes.

S=Provided for in statute R=Provided for in regulations V=Voluntary program; no statute or regulations N=Notice to physicians

	PKU	Hypothyroidism	Galactosemia	Homocystinuria	Maple Syrup Urine Disease	Other Heritable Diseases
Illinois	S, R	S, R	S			S—other metabolic diseases as the department may deem necessary.
Indiana	S, R	S, R				S, R—other inborn errors of metabolism.
Iowa	R	R	R			R—branched chain ketoaciduria.
Kansas	S, R	S, R				S—other such diseases which may be detected by the same procedures.
Kentucky	S, R	R	R			S—other inborn errors of metabolism.
Louisiana	S, R	S, R	S	S	S	S—sickle cell anemia, tyrosinemia
Maine	R	R	R	R	R	S—metabolic abnormalities that may be expected to result in subsequent mental deficiencies. R—other diseases as cost-effective measures become available.
Maryland	R				R	S—any disorder transmitted genetically.
Massachusetts	S					S—cretinism
Michigan	S, R					S, R—other handicapping conditions as the department specifies.
Minnesota	S, R	R	R			S—other inborn errors of metabolism causing mental retardation, as prescribed by the state commissioner of health.

S=Provided for in statute R=Provided for in regulations V=Voluntary program; no statute or regulations N=Notice to physicians

Chart of Newborn Screening Laws—*continued*

	PKU	Hypothyroidism	Galactosemia	Homocystinuria	Maple Syrup Urine Disease	Other Heritable Diseases
Mississippi	S	S				
Missouri	S	R				S—other metabolic defects as the division of health prescribes
Montana	R					S—whichever inborn errors of metabolism the department specifies. R—other aminoacidopathies.
Nebraska	S	S				S—director of health may require tests for other metabolic diseases as they are perfected.
Nevada						S—preventable inheritable disorders leading to mental retardation, specified by the state board of health.
New Hampshire	S, R	N	N	N	N	
New Jersey	S	S	S			S—other preventable biochemical disorders which may cause mental retardation or other permanent disabilities, if reliable and efficient testing for these other disorders is available.
New Mexico	S, R	R	R	R	R	S—other congenital diseases the secretary of health & environment specifies; R—requires sickle-cell anemia testing.
New York	S	S	S	S		S—homozygous sickle cell disease, branched-chain ketonuria, adenosine deaminase deficiency, histindinemia, and such other diseases and conditions as the commissioner may designate.

S=Provided for in statute R=Provided for in regulations V=Voluntary program; no statute or regulations N=Notice to physicians

Chart of Newborn Screening Laws—*continued*

	PKU	Hypothyroidism	Galactosemia	Homocystinuria	Maple Syrup Urine Disease	Other Heritable Diseases
North Carolina	Protocol	Protocol				S--sickle cell and related genetic disorders.
North Dakota	S	Policy statement	Policy statement	Policy statement		S—other inborn errors of metabolism.
Ohio	S	S	S	S		S—if disorder is treatable, will cause disability if untreated, and no additional samples are required.
Oklahoma	S, R	R				S—related inborn metabolic disorders.
Oregon	S, R	R	R		R	S—other metabolic disease. R—hypermethioninemia. R—tyrosinemia.
Pennsylvania	S	R				S—other metabolic disease as advisory health board specifies.
Rhode Island	S, R					
South Carolina	S, R	R				S—inborn metabolic errors.
South Dakota	S	S				S—other metabolic disorders when testing available as the department of health prescribes.
Tennessee	S	S				S—other metabolic defects and disorders likely to cause mental retardation.
Texas	S, R	S, R	R			S—other heritable diseases the board specifies. R—sickling hemoglobinopathies.
Utah	S, R	R	R			S, R—other metabolic diseases.
Vermont	V	V	V			

S=Provided for in statute R=Provided for in regulations V=Voluntary program; no statute or regulations N=Notice to physicians

Chart of Newborn Screening Laws—*continued*

	PKU	Hypothyroidism	Galactosemia	Homocystinuria	Maple Syrup Urine Disease	Other Heritable Diseases
Virginia	S, R	S	S	S	S	S—Other inborn errors of metabolism, and other genetically related diseases, including sickle cell anemia.
Washington	S, R	R				S—Other heritable or metabolic disorders as the board of health specifies.
West Virginia	S	S	S			
Wisconsin	S	S	S		S	S—other metabolic diseases as the dept. of public health directs.
Wyoming	R	R	R	R	R	S—remedial inborn errors of metabolism. R—sickle cell anemia

S=Provided for in statute R=Provided for in regulations V=Voluntary program; no statute or regulations N=Notice to physicians

State Newborn Screening Directors

ALABAMA

Fern Shinbaum
MCH Clinical Director
Family Health Administration
State Department of Public Health
434 Monroe Street
Montgomery, AL 36310
(205) 261-5661

ALASKA

David A. Spence, M.D.
Chief, Family Health Section
Department of Health & Social Services
Health and Welfare Building
Pouch H-06B
Juneau, AK 99811
(907) 465-3107

ARIZONA

Sundin Applegate, M.D.
Bureau of Crippled Children's Services
Arizona Department of Health Services
200 N. Curry Road
Tempe, AZ 85281
(602) 968-6461, ext. 251

ARKANSAS

Earnestine Opovo, M.D., FAAP
Acting Director
Division of Infant and Child Health
State Health Department
4815 West Markham
Little Rock, AR 72201
(501) 661-2476

CALIFORNIA

Virginia L. Mordaunt
Chief, Newborn Screening Section
Genetic Disease Branch
State Department of Health Services
2151 Berkeley Way, Annex 4
Berkeley, CA 94704
(415) 540-2534

COLORADO

Robert S. McCurdy, M.D., M.P.H.
Director
Medical Affairs and Special Programs
State Department of Health
4210 East 11th Avenue
Denver, CO 80220
(303) 320-6137, ext. 422

CONNECTICUT

Vijaya V. Bapat, M.D.
Chief, Maternal and Child Health Section
State Department of Health Services
150 Washington Street
Hartford, CT 06106
(203) 566-4282

DELAWARE

Mary Helen Barrett, R.N., M.S.
Acting Director
Maternal and Child Health
Bureau of Personal Health Services
Division of Public Health
Jesse S. Cooper Memorial Building
Federal and Water Streets
Dover, DE 19901
(302) 736-4785

DISTRICT OF COLUMBIA

Allen F. Calvert, Ph.D.
Division of Medical Genetics
Department of Pediatrics and Child Welfare
Howard University College of Medicine
Washington, D.C. 20059
(202) 636-6380/6340

FLORIDA

Marilyn May, R.N.
Infant Screening Program Coordinator
Department of Health and Services
1317 Winewood Boulevard
Building 5, Room 127
Tallahassee, FL 32301
(904) 487-0588

GEORGIA

Mary Harris, Ph.D.
Director of Genetic Services
Georgia Department of Human Resources
Community Health Section
878 Peachtree Street, Room 202
Atlanta, GA 30309
(404) 656-4850

HAWAII

Darryl Leong, M.D.
Maternal and Child Health Branch
State Department of Health
741-A Sunset Avenue
Honolulu, HI 96816
(808) 548-6554

IDAHO

Mary Jane Webb
Genetics Program Coordinator
Idaho Department of Health and Welfare
2220 Old Penitentiary Road
Boise, ID 83712
(208) 334-4778

ILLINOIS

Sydney Kling, B.S.N., R.N.
Division of Family Health
State Department of Public Health
535 West Jefferson Street
Springfield, IL 62761
(217) 785-4522

INDIANA

F. John Meaney, Ph.D.
Chief, Genetic Diseases Section
Division of Maternal and Child Health
State Board of Health
1330 West Michigan Street
P.O. Box 1964
Indianapolis, IN 46206-1964
(317) 633-0805

IOWA

Roger Chapman, M.S.W.
Administrator
Birth Defects Institute
Iowa State Department of Health
Lucas State Office Building
Des Moines, IA 50319-0075
(515) 281-6646

KANSAS

Carolyn K. Domingo, R.N., M.S.
Genetic Disease Coordinator
Crippled and Chronically Ill
Children's Program
Department of Health and
Environment
Forbes Field
Topeka, KS 66620
(913) 862-9360, ext. 400

KENTUCKY

Patricia K. Nicol, M.D., M.P.H.
Director for Metabolic Screening
Department of Health Services
Cabinet for Human Resources
275 East Main Street
Frankfort, KY 40621
(502) 564-4430

LOUISIANA

Cora R. Charles, R.N., M.N.
Genetic Nurse Consultant
Department of Health and
Human Resources
Office of Health Services and
Environmental Quality
P.O. Box 60630
New Orleans, LA 70160
(504) 568-5075

MAINE

Ibrahim Parvanta, M.S.
Director, Newborn Screening
Program
Division of Maternal and Child
Health
Department of Human Services
State House, Station 11
Augusta, ME 04333
(207) 289-3311

MARYLAND

Susan Panny, M.D.
Chief, Division of Hereditary
Disorders
State Department of Health and
Hygiene
201 West Preston Street
Baltimore, MD 21201
(301) 383-6321

MASSACHUSETTS

Marvin L. Mitchell, M.D.
Director
New England Regional Newborn
Screening Program
State Laboratory Institute
State Department of Public Health
Jamaica Plain, MA 02130
(617) 522-3700, ext. 160

MICHIGAN

Bill Young, Ph.D.
Genetic Program Coordinator
Division of Maternal and
Child Health
Bureau of Health Promotion and
Disease Prevention
State Department of Public Health
3500 North Logan Street
P.O. Box 30035
Lansing, MI 48909
(517) 373-0657

MINNESOTA

Dwayne Morse, Dr. P.H.
Director, Medical Laboratories
State Department of Health
717 Delaware Street, S.E.
P.O. Box 9441
Minneapolis, MN 55440
(612) 623-5241

MISSISSIPPI

Daniel R. Bender
Director
Genetics Project
State Department of Health
P.O. Box 1700
Jackson, MS 39215-1700
(601) 982-6571

MISSOURI

Winford L. Jenkins
State Coordinator for Metabolic Screening
Bureau of Family Health Care
Division of Health
Department of Social Services
1730 East Elm
Jefferson City, MO 65101
(314) 751-4667

MONTANA

Sidney Pratt, M.D., Chief
Clinical Programs Bureau
Health Services and Medical Facilities Division
Department of Health and Environmental Sciences
Cogswell Building
Helena, MT 59620
(406) 444-4740

NEBRASKA

Robert S. Grant, M.D., M.P.H.
Medical Director
Maternal and Child Health Division
State Department of Health
301 Centennial Mall South, 3rd Floor
P.O. Box 95007
Lincoln, NE 68509
(402) 471-2907

NEVADA

Richard Bentinck, M.D.
Bureau Chief
Bureau of Community Health Services
505 East King, Room 205
Carson City, NV 89710
(702) 885-4885

NEW HAMPSHIRE

Concetta A. Cucinotta, M.S.
Newborn Screening Coordinator
Bureau of Handicapped Children
Health and Welfare Building
Hazen Drive
Concord, NH 03301
(603) 271-4528

NEW JERSEY

Yaovares Thatsneyakul, M.D.
Coordinator, Medical Service
Special Child Health Services Program
NJ State Department of Health
CN 364
Trenton, NJ 08625
(609) 984-0775

NEW MEXICO

Ian Buchanan
Newborn Genetic Screening Program
Scientific Laboratory Division
700 Camino De Salud, N.E.
Albuquerque, NM 87106
(505) 841-2581

NEW YORK

Thomas P. Carter, Ph.D.
Director, Newborn Screening Program
Laboratory of Human Genetics
Wadsworth Center for Laboratories
and Research
State Department of Health
Empire State Plaza
Albany, NY 12201
(518) 473-7552

NORTH CAROLINA

Elizabeth Moore
Director Genetics Program
Division of Health Services
Department of Human Resources
P.O. Box 2091
Raleigh, NC 27602
(919) 733-7437

NORTH DAKOTA

Robert M. Wentz, M.D., M.P.H.
Director
Division of Maternal and Child
Health
State Department of Health
Capitol Building
Bismarck, ND 58505
(701) 224-2493

OHIO

Virginia Miller, R.N., M.P.H, M.S.
State Department of Health
P.O. Box 118
246 North High Street
Columbus, OH 43216
(614) 466-4644

OKLAHOMA

Edd D. Rhoades, M.D.
Director, Pediatric Division
State Department of Health
1000 N.E. 10th Street
P.O. Box 53551
Oklahoma City, OK 73152
(405) 271-4471

OREGON

Rhesa L. Penn, M.D., M.P.H.
Medical Consultant
Oregon State Health Division
P.O. Box 231
Portland, OR 97207
(503) 229-6390

PENNSYLVANIA

C. Gail Stock
Director, Neonatal Metabolic
Screening Program
State Department of Health
P.O. Box 90
Harrisburg, PA 17108
(717) 787-7440

PUERTO RICO

Pedro J. Santiago-Borrero, M.D.
Director
Genetic Diseases Screening Program
University Children's Hospital
University of Puerto Rico Medical
School
G.P.O. Box 5067
San Juan, Puerto Rico 00936
(809) 765-2363

RHODE ISLAND

Raymond G. Lundgren, Ph.D.
Health Laboratory Building
State Department of Health
50 Orms Street
Providence, RI 02904
(401) 274-1011

SOUTH CAROLINA

Marilyn C. Moody
Assistant Project Director
Maternal and Child Health Division
State Department of Health and Environmental Control
2600 Bull Street
Columbia, SC 29201
(803) 758-5533

SOUTH DAKOTA

Allen W. Krom, M.S.W.
Health Services Assistant Administrator
Division of Health Services
State Department of Health
523 East Capitol
Pierre, SD 57501
(605) 773-3737

TENNESSEE

Dorothy Turner, M.D.
Program Director
Maternal and Child Health
State Department of Health and Environment
One Hundred 9th Avenue North, 3rd Floor
Nashville, TN 37219-5405
(615) 741-7335

TEXAS

Lois O. Brown, R.N.
Coordinator
Newborn Screening Program
Bureau of Maternal and Child Health
Texas Department of Health
1100 West 49th Street
Austin, TX 78756
(512) 458-7700

UTAH

Glorya Garcia Schow, R.N.
Genetic Nurse Consultant
Division of Family Health Services
State Department of Health
44 Medical Drive
Salt Lake City, UT 84113
(801) 533-4084

VERMONT

Richard A. Aronson, M.D.
Director
Medical Services Division
State Department of Health
1193 North Avenue
P.O. Box 70
Burlington, VT 05402
(802) 862-5701, ext. 365

VIRGINIA

Arlethia Rogers, R.N.
Genetic Metabolic Nurse Coordinator
State Department of Health
Bureau of Maternal and Child Health
109 Governor Street, Room 624
Richmond, VA 23219
(804) 786-7367

WASHINGTON

H.C. Thuline, M.D., Head
Genetic Services Section
Department of Social and Health
Services
1704 N.E. 150th Street
Seattle, WA 98155
(206) 545-6783

WEST VIRGINIA

Mary S. Skinner, M.D.
Division of Maternal and Child Health
State Department of Health
1143 Dunbar Avenue
Dunbar, WV 25064
(304) 766-0250

WISCONSIN

Ron Laessig, Ph.D.
Director
State Laboratory of Hygiene
465 Henry Mall
Madison, WI 53706
(608) 262-1293

WYOMING

R. Larry Meuli, M.D., F.A.A.P.
Director, Family Health Services
Department of Health and Social
Services
Hathaway Building
Cheyenne, WY 82002
(307) 777-6297